How To Deal With Crazy People

The Ultimate Survival Guide On How To Deal With the Psychopath, Sociopath, Narcissist And Other Disturbed People

By James Wilcox

I0412989

Table of Contents

Introduction

We have all seen them—the people who walk to the beat of a different drummer. We have shook our heads and wondered just what they were thinking and why they engage in this behavior. We have puzzled over their behaviors, questioned them, and in some cases asked them to stop an annoying behavior, but they quickly fall right back into the same patterns. It is great when we can watch from afar and not have to deal with these unusual people or we can just close-up shop and walk the other way, but unfortunately, these people are a part of our world and cannot be avoided.

These "crazy" people could be in our immediate families or at work. We encounter them at school and at the store, no matter where we go we cannot avoid their unusual mannerisms, odd views, and somewhat eccentric behaviors. But even though we may not be able to avoid them, there are strategies that we can use to better understand and deal with them. Through the next several pages we will look at examples of a multitude of different behaviors, how to recognize them and deal with them in day to day situations. We will discuss famous personalities who have learned to deal with their psychological differences. We will also look at the symptoms, treatments, and strategies for how to deal with these "crazy" people in our lives.

In every person's life they will have encountered someone who fell well outside the accepted norms and behaviors that we expect from people in our lives; the people that we looked at twice trying our best to understand what they were doing and the motivations for their actions. These are psychopaths and sociopaths that display behaviors that fall outside of the norms that are typically accepted by society. When they do something unusual, they will typically show no remorse for their actions, even if they broke the law. They may even repeat those actions despite the risk of punishment or repercussion as a result of their actions. These highly evolved people are often very intelligent and exude charm; and they appear to truly care as they draw people into their world.

This type of irrational person can put our lives, our children's lives, and even the lives of friends and family members at stake due to their actions. There are many examples of famous psychopaths and sociopaths throughout history who have led people astray and then performed a variety of very serious crimes against them, making them operate well on the fringes of society. We will examine how to recognize this type of personality and how to identify the warning signs leading to the concept that someone may be a little off balance in their behavior and manner of thinking towards other people.

Another personality type that can be exceptionally difficult to deal with is someone who has a narcissistic personality disorder. When we consider the case of someone with this disorder and who struggles to form meaningful relationships with anyone but themselves, we will better understand how to deal with this type of person and their special needs within society. This type of person constantly seeks the attention and admiration of others and will be upset or lash out when they do not receive the attention that they think they deserve. This type of person will struggle throughout life looking for the approval of others and be very disappointed when he/she finally realizes that the world does not revolve around them and their needs. Narcissists will have a difficult time with any meaningful relationships and will appear haughty and unreachable emotionally, yet their constant need for praise and admiration only hides a real insecurity inside, which they try to conceal from everyone around them. If someone that you know struggles with this condition we will offer tips to manage the relationship so that they can be dealt with kindly and in a way that they will be able to handle.

Bipolar disorder has become more prevalent in society as a whole as many famous personalities report suffering from this condition. The sometimes violent mood swings that someone with bipolar disorder faces can disrupt their day-to-day life, making it extremely difficult for them to function in society as a whole. Many bipolar disorder sufferers can become reclusive while they try and manage the issues that they are facing due to their disorder. In the early stages of this disease, a person with bipolar disorder can often become very confused about what is happening to them and how their life is being disrupted by their symptoms. Bipolar disorder is highly treatable and many with this condition have learned how to deal with their mental imbalances; they have successfully received treatment and continued on to recover and lead highly successful lives despite their condition. In later pages we will discuss the symptoms of bipolar disorder, when to seek treatment, and how to manage interpersonal relationships with someone who has this condition.

Another disorder that can affect people who suffered a traumatic event in their childhood is multiple personality disorder. While this condition has been portrayed in many horror and psychic thrillers where one of the hidden personalities ends up being a psychotic killer, this actual disorder does exist, but not to the extreme degree that it is portrayed in movies. This condition can result when a child forms distinct personalities in response to a traumatic event during their personality formative years. When someone displays this condition they will have a completely different persona, amnesia, or may walk around in a haze not noticing or able to interact with those around them. There are multiple different manifestations of this psychological issue and it can be managed with therapy and supportive treatment.

Neuroses and neurotic behaviors are very common and just about everyone has some type of neuroses that they give in to throughout their adult lives. Often these neuroses develop based on an earlier event in their life that caused them trauma or injury such as falling off a bike or being in an accident. When these people are faced with the same event later in life, they may show an unreasonable fear of the event resulting in them not wanting to take part or to avoid the situation in case it could happen again. Many have thought that neuroses developed as a safety mechanism to protect ourselves from injury and that in some cases, the brain goes into overdrive staying safe and avoiding situations that are even remotely similar to the situation where they were injured previously.

If you want to know more about random diseases, then consider talking about them with a hypochondriac. No matter how rare or obscure the disease may be, hypochondriacs will often think that they are suffering from this disease.

This condition causes them to constantly worry about their health, causing them to suspect they have a multitude of diseases and conditions; therefore, they are in constant need of treatment. Often, they avoid contact with other people for fear of catching something or picking up their germs and will take numerous steps to avoid getting sick or catching something. Hypochondriacs will constantly come up with new diseases and conditions and may create elaborate treatment methods and routines that they must follow to avoid catching a disease or becoming ill. There are strategies that can help to manage these hypochondriac symptoms, but when it comes down to it, hypochondriacs can be challenging people to deal with in our day-to-day lives.

Another disorder that can seriously impact a person's life and how they interact with the people around them is post-traumatic stress disorder. This more serious condition exists for many returning from war zones causing families, friends, and co-workers to have to face this difficult to manage disorder. This serious condition faces many soldiers who return from war zones, but also can happen to everyday people who experience a traumatizing event in their lives. PTSD is a serious condition that requires treatment, support and understanding from everyone around the person in order for them to learn how to better integrate in society and resume their lives after the traumatic event. PTSD is a difficult, but treatable condition that requires therapy with multiple resources that can help people suffering from this condition to learn how to adjust to their symptoms and still lead a productive life with healthy relationships.

Do you know someone in your life who habitually avoids contact with other people? If this becomes a regular debilitating pattern, then they just might be suffering from avoidant personality disorder. This condition will make people extremely reluctant to engage in society and they will have overwhelming feelings of shyness and inadequacy that will prevent them from interacting with other people. This is more than just your average shyness; people suffering from this disorder will have a serious debilitation which prevents them from being a part of society as a whole. There are treatments and therapies available to help people with this disorder, as well as strategies for friends, families, and co-workers to use to help them better interact with these types of individuals.

Another type of personality disorder that can be seen within society is borderline personality disorder. This condition causes people to constantly act impulsively without any regard for the consequences or negative perceptions of their actions. They will display this type of behavior over a period of time to where it becomes habitual and they will find that they cannot control their impulses, often ending up in trouble with the law. People can learn to manage these symptoms but the key is to recognize them and get treatment early before they irreparably damage their life, career, and family.

Schizotypal personality disorder is another condition that many people will face within their daily lives and someone you may know may be suffering from this condition. This disorder is characterized by an extreme or unhealthy need for social isolation and the tendency to have a slightly different view on reality than other people within society. People with this condition will often avoid forming any meaningful relationships and will often have unusual modes of speaking and dress that will separate them from others. They will frequently have a different view on reality than other people and may believe in the paranormal and other abnormal ideas. Managing these symptoms is possible and with assistance and treatment they can learn to interact with society, be employed, and have a family or other relationships.

Have you ever had someone say they would do something, then roll their eyes as they walk away never to do what they said that they would? While this may seem unusual, this type of behavior is an example of passive aggressive behavior. These behaviors show up in people who have a difficult time confronting people and addressing conflicts directly, but instead take a passive approach to show they are displeased. Dealing with this behavior and managing it can be difficult, but with understanding and help people can learn to address issues in a healthier manner and to not fall into passive aggressive behaviors.

Eating is an essential part of life, but when people have issues regarding the food they take in, then this normal day-to-day activity becomes an exercise in futility. Sometimes there is a basis for why a person eats the foods that they do, but other times it is just a frustrating choice. Food and eating related issues can negatively impact social interactions in a group setting and people may become uncomfortable or display unusual behaviors that may lead others to suspect that they are not quite right. Serious health conditions can result when someone has poor eating habits or binges and then purges their food and they must seek medical attention. With treatment and counseling they can learn proper and healthy eating habits and eliminate some of the side effects that result.

Mild autism is becoming more prevalent in society as people constantly are being diagnosed and falling on the autism spectrum. The autism spectrum is a scale that helps to measure the degree to which people display the symptoms of autism and helps to better classify and understand the issues they are facing. Mild autism will generally show up in our day-to-day interactions with people both at home, school, and the workplace when you see different or unusual responses to situations; unfortunately, there are many who go undiagnosed, but may actually fall on the autism spectrum. When you encounter someone who does not respond like others do, they just might fall on the autism spectrum and have an entirely different perspective on life that others may not always understand. Included in this book are strategies for identifying someone with this disorder and ways to better understand them and how they interact with the world.

Many people will suffer from depression at some point in their lives, but when it becomes debilitating then they will want to seek professional help to work through their issue. Depression can come on due to a life event or a medical condition, but it can be successfully treated and managed if you are able to get help with this condition. Family and friends are a big part in the treatment for depression as they will be able to work with their loved one to find the appropriate medical treatment to cope with this disease.

Have you ever seen someone who just cannot sit still? Or that moves from topic to topic without any direction or focus? This type of condition is a medical conditional known as Attention Deficit and Hyperactivity Disorder and is frequently seen in all areas of society that we come in contact with. People suffering from ADHD will have problems in their daily lives focusing on the topic at hand and will jump randomly to a new activity, rarely finishing anything that they started.

Finally, Obsessive Compulsive Disorder or OCD is another condition that people face in their everyday lives. People with this condition will often have a routine they must go through each day and will experience stress if they do not complete that routine. This is a difficult condition for some to deal with and many people will have some form of OCD in varying degrees.

There are a multitude of different types of people who fall into the broad category of "crazy" and when you understand what these types are you will be better prepared to manage the multitude of "crazy" personalities ahead of you. In this book, we will explore the different types of personalities that you will encounter every day and provide a better understanding of each of these disorders. When you understand the personalities, their quirks and their idiosyncrasies, you will be better able to manage them and be effective while maintaining your own sanity in the meantime.

Chapter 1: Tips for Managing a Relationship with a Psychopath

Psychopath. When we read or hear that word it can cause us to cringe. This word that describes those people who live and function on the outskirts of society and who display behavior that is not socially acceptable within normal bounds of society. We hear about the psychopath serial killers who watch for their prey then perform unspeakable acts and take people's lives. Psychopaths are sometimes difficult to catch because they are withdrawn from society as a whole, but when they do engage with society they will appear charming and easy to get along with on the surface, yet underneath the surface they lack any empathy for other human beings. This Jekyll and Hyde personality can be difficult for people to understand which makes them generally disturbing and uncomfortable for people to be around.

It can be frightening to consider that there are psychopaths walking among us every day. While they may not always perform the despicable acts that are depicted in Hollywood movies or on television shows, they exhibit behaviors that are not socially acceptable and walk a fine line of being illegal. A psychopath is similar to a sociopath, who we will describe in the next section of this book. A psychopath perceives and interacts with situations in a way that is dysfunctional, as does a sociopath, and they both will have no regard for what is right or wrong. People who are sociopaths and psychopaths are more likely to break the law and seriously harm or kill another human being.

What is a Psychopath?

The term psychopath has been used for over two hundred years to describe a personality disorder where the person will appear outwardly normal, but has a sense of moral depravity on their day-to-day personal interactions. Their actions will demonstrate no emotional connection with other human beings, which can make them impervious to the results, consequences, and outcomes of their actions.

Psychopaths can, and do, intermingle and adjust to living and working within society which makes them more concerning when we try to deal with them in our everyday lives. If you watch for the signs and monitor behaviors, though, you will be able to identify if someone that you know could be classified as a psychopath and take steps to better deal with that person and understand their behaviors.

Psychopath Description

A psychopath is defined as someone who suffers from any type of mental disorder that will often manifest itself in violent or severely antisocial behaviors. People with this type of disorder are defined as lunatics, psychotic, or egocentric and will often struggle to establish any type of personal relationships. A psychopath falls under the umbrella of a variety of antisocial personality disorders and is a constant, chronic condition.

The description of a psychopath is used very often in legal terminology and criminology to describe a set of antisocial and criminal actions. It will also frequently be used in movies and television to depict disturbed individuals who commit a variety of heinous crimes. When someone hears the word psychopath, they almost instantly think of someone evil that could potentially harm them as a result of these depictions.

Medical Considerations
The medical diagnosis for a psychopath places this disorder under the group of antisocial personality disorders which have been medically proven to have a biological cause. The brain of a person with this condition lacks the synapsis that connects to the emotional part of their brain giving them a complete lack of emotion. Because they do not feel the same emotional response that normal human beings will feel, they will have a complete disregard for what is right and wrong and will perform heinous acts with no remorse. Likewise, they will use charm or wit to

influence others for a multitude of reasons and feel no guilt for using and manipulating other people.

Symptoms to watch for when dealing with a psychopath will be a lack of emotional connection with their environment, a tendency to exploit others for their own personal gain, acting very charming and manipulative, having a sense of superiority, or displaying very hostile and agitated behaviors. They will say things that are inappropriate or at the wrong times and not seem to care for people who are injured, disabled, or sick. There are different degrees of psychopathy and some doctors have gone so far as to say that a psychopath, or mild psychopathy, can be a result of how a person was raised.

When a psychopath engages in an activity, they lack the ability to modulate their actions and feelings based on the information being presented in their environment. When you compare a normal functioning person to a psychopath, the normal person will adjust their behaviors to match social norms, but a psychopath does not make this adjustment and their reactions will seem uncaring or inappropriate.

For example, when a normal functioning person enters a hospital to visit a sick patient, they will demonstrate compassion and concern for the care of the sick patient. However, the psychopath will not adjust their tone for the situation and may be seen telling jokes about the sick person's hospital treatment or side effects and demonstrate a complete lack of concern for the patient. Since a psychopath lacks the connections in their brain to create and to process the emotions that result from these actions, they will not understand why people are offended and will continue the behaviors. These actions will alienate others and cause considerable harm to their interpersonal relationships.

Typical Behaviors
Psychopaths will often demonstrate a complete disregard for what other people consider right and wrong and will show a lack of concern for breaking the law. They will tend to rarely tell the truth and will use deceit to get the best of other people or get them to do what they want. A psychopath will be a master at becoming "prince charming" when they want someone to do something for them, but can have violent mood swings if things do not go their way. They will tend to act as if they are superior to all others around them and will be very egocentric in their conversations. Some psychopaths will have constant issues with breaking the law and run-ins with law enforcement, but then they will use their charm and wit to manipulate the system to their advantage. Many psychopaths will constantly take part in very risky or dangerous

behaviors that put their safety and the safety of those around them in jeopardy.

Psychopaths will struggle at maintaining healthy relationships with other people which many doctors relate to issues of neglect and abuse when they were a child. These issues will continue throughout their life making psychopaths typically loners who operate on the fringes of society.

When you speak with a psychopath you will tend to get a sense that they are insincere in their words. Sometimes they will be overly superficial in what they are saying or have a superficial feeling to everything they say. When they speak there is no feeling behind the words, which makes people doubt that they are sincere and suspect they are not telling the truth. This makes developing a meaningful relationship with a psychopath very difficult as they can easily tell a straight face lie as easily as if they were telling someone that they loved them. Relationships with a psychopath, as a result, are difficult to form, as you can never tell for certain if the person truly means what they are saying.

A psychopath will rarely accept responsibility for their actions and will blame others for things that were not actually their fault. They refuse to accept the consequences of their actions and will not demonstrate any shame or remorse for what they have done. This makes any type of rehabilitation difficult that is why psychopaths will typically have run-ins with the law and will be in and out of jail frequently.

One concerning trait of a psychopath is their tendency towards violence. Their violent actions are a result of their lack of tolerance for any type of frustration. When they become frustrated they tend to lash out at those around them and will show a tendency to want to get in physical fights with other people or will assault people when they become frustrated. This form of aggression can be difficult to manage and those around them may frequently be injured.

Finally, people who are psychopaths tend to have a difficult time obtaining and keeping a job so it is unlikely, but still a possibility, that you will find them in the workplace. Often they will go from job to job, but due to the issues of their condition they will very frequently be unable to keep a job. Psychopaths, on a more extreme level, will avoid finding work altogether and have a difficult time considering the future and choose to live in the present with no concern for how they will support themselves later in life.

Example of a Psychopath
There have been many psychopaths throughout history who have made a very big impact on society in a very frightening manner. For example, Josef Mengele was a notorious doctor during World War II who was a notable

psychopath. He personally was responsible for hundreds of thousands of deaths during that time frame and conducted medical experiments on patients that many would find quite atrocious. Also during the World War II, there was another example of a psychopath in the notorious German leader, Adolf Hitler. He is known as one of the most evil leaders in the history of humans. Adolf Hitler clearly demonstrated one of the traits of a psychopath by being able to win over followers with a charming personality and getting them to perform terrible acts for him. He was the image of a madman in control and was directly responsible for the violent deaths of millions upon millions of innocent men, women, and children in which he showed no remorse, emotion, or care. Hitler's actions were the definition of a psychopath's.

Strategies to be Effective (Family, Co-workers, Friends, Random Encounters)

Having a family member who is diagnosed with an antisocial personality disorder can be a challenge for the entire family and in particular the stigma of having a psychopath to "care for" can be very debilitating. There are two parts of dealing with a family member with these issues: first is helping a young child to learn how to behave when they are missing the important parts of their brain that give them an emotional tie to other family members and learn to deal with right, wrong, and appropriate behaviors. The second part, for an older person who has been diagnosed with this condition, is learning to manage the condition and helping them to participate in society in a positive and appropriate manner.

Consider the movie "The Good Son" which demonstrated the difference between two young boys, one whom was a normal boy and the other a psychopath. The good boy regularly went about his day doing things that normal children did; however, he also tried to stop his psychopathic brother from harming others. Unfortunately, the good son's noble intentions were reversed and then pinned on him when the psychopathic brother turned on his charm for their parents. While this movie displayed an extreme case of a psychopathic personality in a child, it did demonstrate the charming behaviors that can fool a parent into thinking that their child is good. There are signs to watch for, however, in children. Young children will tend to be withdrawn emotionally and speak in an unusually calm voice for a child.

Most children, as they grow and develop, will over emphasize the emotion in their voice as they learn to control their emotions, but a young child who does not have these emotional links in their brain will not need to learn this control. Another behavior to watch for in children is constantly blaming others for their actions. Now, this behavior is normal in children as they try to avoid punishment, but with a child with psychopathic tendencies they will go through elaborate stories pinning this action on another child while tending to charm their way out of a situation. Another behavior to monitor is frustration and violent actions. If a child is struggling with a problem and is unable to solve it they will tend to lash out and hit another person or a family pet. These actions must be curbed and redirected early in their life.

With successful parenting, a child with these tendencies can learn the difference between right and wrong and can channel their feelings in a productive manner. Parents and family members need to work as a group to help the child learn, but must understand that the child's brain does not work the same as everyone else's and they must be patient and understanding at all times when their responses seem inappropriate.

Adult family members with a psychopathic diagnosis will need more intervention. While there are no specific medications that treat this issue there are medications that can help with other symptoms such as the depression or aggressive tendencies. Psychotherapy is key for these adults to help them to deal with their issues, but often their symptoms prevent them from accepting responsibility for what they are doing making them difficult to manage through treatment. Often family members will also require therapy to find help and support managing their loved one and helping with their care.

It is unlikely that you will encounter a psychopath in the work force, but highly functioning people with this disorder could show up. If someone has learned to control their symptoms enough to be engaged in society then you may encounter them. Psychopaths can show up in highly technical arenas or the medical profession where they are able to work in solitude and have little engagement with others. They will typically be found in arenas where human connections are not required in order to be successful at their job.

Random encounters are more likely with a psychopath as you go about your daily life so be sure to watch for the signs and symptoms when you encounter these people to avoid being charmed into doing something you otherwise would not feel right doing.

Chapter 2: Tips for Managing a Relationship with a Sociopath

Have you ever been to a party and seen one person dominating the conversation? This person would often have a superficial charm that drew people into the group and got them included in an often risky activity. Or have you ever known that one person, who seemed to take delight in hurting small animals or picking on others until they left in tears? These types of people will fall under the umbrella of a sociopath.

While it can be easy to avoid the homes of sociopaths who isolate themselves in their own little worlds, there are sociopaths that we must interact with in society and these are the group that we need a strategy to deal with in order to better manage our interactions with them on a regular basis.

What is a Sociopath?

A sociopath is someone who exhibits a variety of different types of antisocial behavior. This could include intentionally driving someone from their lives or their personal space all the way up to criminal behaviors such as rape and murder. Sociopaths have no sense of what socially acceptable behavior is and lack any sort of understanding as to what is right and wrong, especially in regards to other human beings.

Within the wirings of our brain, most human beings, and even animals in the animal kingdom, will have an inherent trait or an integral bit of programming that is hardwired into their brains that prevents them from killing another member of their own species. But within the brain of a sociopath they lack this wiring and they will feel no remorse at committing heinous acts towards another human being and will inflict pain and torture without feeling that they are doing anything wrong. This type of antisocial behavior can be difficult to manage when you encounter one in your daily life and risky to society as a whole.

Sociopath Description
Sociopath and psychopath are often confused for one another when it comes to personality disorders. A sociopath is essentially a type of psychopath, but the antisocial behavior that sociopaths display is many times criminal in nature and this type of person will have no sense of moral responsibility towards others or towards society as a whole.

Sociopaths will tend to operate well outside the established societal norms and demonstrate no moral compass or sense of social responsibility. They typically shun contact with society and live in their own world and their own reality until their most despicable acts that have robbed someone of their life or liberty are discovered and they are finally brought to justice. They have a tendency to tell straight faced lies while displaying no emotion or speak with no outward expression or noticeable feeling of guilt. When they speak the truth or a lie they will appear exactly the same and will use the exact same tone for both. The will rarely have long-standing loving relationships or may cheat on partners they choose to be with. Sociopaths are often highly intelligent and able to do well in work if they choose to, but can be prone to influencing others to take part in illegal or questionable activities.

Most of all, sociopaths are egocentric and like to be the center of attention when they engage in society and with others.

Medical Considerations
Sociopaths typically demonstrate very antisocial behaviors and are interested only in what they want or desire with no consideration for others or how what they want could impact others.

When diagnosing whether or not a person is a sociopath, doctors and psychiatrists will consider the following questions:

First, does the person seem very charming and highly intelligent, yet very superficial? Sociopaths are often able to charm the people around them and draw them into a group or conversation; this alluring nature draws the unsuspecting victim into the sociopath's web, allowing them to be manipulated and often controlled by the sociopath into doing whatever the sociopath would like them to do.

A second consideration when a person could be a sociopath is if they are unreliable. Sociopaths do not have the normal considerations for others so they are not compelled to follow through on social engagements. If you know a person who tends to be unreliable and regularly misses engagements with no apology for being late, then they could fall under the category of a sociopath.

Sociopaths will rarely show any forms of guilt or shame no matter what they have done. From the small act of missing a birthday party for a family member to the larger criminal acts of famous sociopaths who murdered one or more people (sometimes even cannibalizing their remains), they never appear to show that they feel bad for their actions.

Another consideration on whether a person is a sociopath is whether or not they appear nervous or suffer from any types of neuroses. A sociopath is rational and will appear confident even when taking what others consider to be a risk. They never appear nervous or anxious no matter what they are doing and can discuss these actions with the same unattached and emotional responses.

Next, a sociopath will always be super rational in their thoughts and actions and they will never be delusional. They will always appear to be completely in touch with the world around them and not be prone to thoughts of grandeur. They very rarely display emotions and will constantly appear cold and calculated in all of their actions. They can appear robotic, and generally do not respond as people would normally anticipate would be appropriate for a situation.

Habitual liars or people that typically speak in an insincere manner may fall under the description of a sociopath. This type of behavior is very typical of a sociopath as they are quite comfortable lying if the truth is not what suits them. Sociopaths will tell a lie as easily as other people tell the truth and there will be no outward indication that they are lying while they are speaking. When sociopaths speak, you will constantly feel that they do not truly believe what they are saying.

Another consideration for a sociopath is if they randomly demonstrate antisocial behavior. Sociopaths will often act in an unacceptable manner with little or no provocation and their actions will seem to be way out of proportion to what is going on around them. These behaviors will make everyone in the group uncomfortable, but the sociopath will simply charm their way out of the situation until they become the life of the party again.

Many sociopaths will repeatedly make the same mistake over and over and never learn from their actions and punishments. Many will be incarcerated numerous times for the same offense and never change their ways as a result. The jail system is full of sociopaths who match this description and, unfortunately, is not prepared to deal with the psychological help that these inmates truly need to not become repeat offenders.

A large amount of sociopaths are egocentric and not capable of forming loving, long-term relationships with another human being. They will typically be loners who only pull people into their circle when they want to manipulate or use them. Even typical behaviors such as loving a parent will be foreign for a sociopath as they will not be capable of forming that emotional connection or bond with their family.

One disturbing trait of a sociopath is that use deception so that they fit in with society as a whole. Sociopaths have learned to fake their responses in order to fit in with a social group, almost in an effort to camouflage their behaviors and to not be spotted or singled out as a sociopath.

Finally, sociopaths will often have a difficult time holding down a job as it requires a long term commitment to another person. Since sociopaths do not feel the need to meet others expectations or feel guilt when they let someone down, they will typically struggle with employment, unless they have excelled to a level where they work independently. Sociopaths may show up in research environments where they work alone and away from other people.

All of these considerations are made in order to diagnose a person as a sociopath and people can demonstrate these behaviors in varying degrees throughout their lives.

Typical Behaviors

Sociopaths can be difficult to spot as they often are able to blend in with society when they choose to engage with other human beings. Because of the similarities with psychopathy, a sociopath also is able to charm other people and draw in unsuspecting people into their own world to use as they see fit. Sociopaths will often be very sexy, good-looking, attractive, and beguiling. They will have traits that draw other people into their circle allowing the sociopath to manipulate them as they see fit. The sociopath will come across as a very exciting personality often with stories and tales of escapades that many people would be afraid to try, but are very exciting to listen to and share in their experiences. Many times a sociopath will be the life of the party and will be leaders in many activities that get people involved. These behaviors will typically be displayed by people at the low end of the sociopath scale who have not crossed over the line into criminal activity which can also occur.

When a sociopath crosses the line into activity that is criminal in nature, their motivations are to take advantage of people who are seen as weaker than them. Often a sociopath will start out with small, socially unacceptable behaviors such as killing small animals or letting small helpless animals die when they could easily be rescued. They begin to take pleasure in these activities and they develop a need for more.

They often will think or dream about killing those who are close to them, but may still be able to refrain from taking action on these thoughts. Many sociopaths struggle internally with their condition and will hide their symptoms from others. In many cases, the condition can be difficult to diagnose as they can easily hide their symptoms and charm their way out of a situation.

Example of a Sociopath
There are many examples of sociopaths within our society such as the famous serial killer Jeffrey Dahmer. Dahmer was notorious for having raped, and murdered over 17 men and

boys. There were other serial killers such as Ted Bundy who killed anywhere between 40 and 100 women before he was stopped and convicted. John Wayne Gacy, murdered over 33 teenage boys and men, was also considered a sociopath. All of the other aforementioned men were also considered psychopaths as well.

Charles Manson is another example of a famous sociopath who used his charming ways to convince others to torture and kill for him. There are religious leaders who fall in the sociopath category such as Tony Alamo, who used his ministry to trap and perform sex acts on children; or more recently the leader Warren Jeffs who used his influence over his religious community to perform spiritual marriages with under-aged girls and have sex with them until he was finally captured and incarcerated to protect his victims and punish him for his misdeeds.

Sociopaths regularly prey on society and can be in other arenas as well, such as those who work in businesses and convince people to invest large sums of money into failing investments and eventually stealing their money. For example, the businessman Sheldon Adelson was a casino mogul and CEO of Las Vegas Sands Corporation that supported right wing groups in both the United States and Israel. He is considered one of the most corrupt businessmen in the world and would regularly funnel funds into whatever country, cause or campaign he wanted to influence. This example displays how sociopaths use the ability to charm people and draw them into criminal behavior with no regard for morality.

Strategies to be Effective (Family, Co-workers, Friends, Random Encounters)

Dealing with a family member who is diagnosed as a sociopath can be challenging for the entire family unit. First and foremost, the family will typically struggle with the fact that their loved one does not respond in the manner that they anticipate. They will appear cold and uncaring as if they have no compassion towards the family itself. In the case of a child, it is difficult for a mother and a father to think that their child does not love them, but in reality the child does not have the connections within their brain to form those bonds. This should not stop the parent from expressing love to the child, but they must not be put off when the child does not respond in the manner they think is appropriate.

Children who have a sociopathic disorder will not respond to a request of "do it for your mother" and will have no urge to please their parents. They will also not feel guilty for doing something wrong, nor will punishments be effective, as the child does not have a moral compass that drives them to do what is right and avoid doing what is wrong. Remember that sociopaths, even as children, are driven to gain power and not praise, so the things that motivate them are different than other children.

Dealing with an adult sociopathic family member is similar to a child, but they will now have more established behaviors. Adults will still try to gain the upper hand and be more powerful in the relationship by trying to gain something such as money or power that they hold over the other person. They will still seem superficial and not have meaningful bonds with their family which can be difficult to understand. They will often remain single throughout their lives since they do not typically form loving relationships or if they do marry they may tend to cheat and feel no remorse for having betrayed their partners.

Dealing with a sociopath in a work situation can be more challenging. Imagine being employed in one of the businesses led by a famous sociopath who was later arrested and charged with a crime. These famous sociopaths led their companies and customers to ruin using their charming personalities and abilities to lie outright to get people to do what they wanted them to do. When working in a company led by a sociopath or someone you think may be doing something illegal, then it is essential to document your work and protect yourself so that you are not framed for any illegal activities. If you see illegal activities you must leave and report them as soon as possible or risk being involved in the activity as an accomplice and possibly face jail time or prosecution.

Everyone has probably encountered a sociopath in their lifetime from certain friends who were always taking part in risky activities to random encounters with someone who was the life of the party and drew everyone around them into their circle. With each of these encounters it is key to not be drawn into their web and to maintain your own moral compass on what is right and wrong. Their world will seem exciting, but you will find that the consequences can be steep for their actions and you will suffer in the end if you do not say no.

Chapter 3: Tips for Managing a Relationship with a Narcissist

Have you ever gone into a public restroom and seen someone stand there primping and admiring themselves in the mirror? Or walked down the street and come close to bumping into someone who was preoccupied with looking at their reflection in the mirror and not watching where they were going? In each of these examples, these personalities are more interested in admiring themselves than paying attention to what is going on in the world around them as they gaze at their reflected image.

You may not believe it, but it is true. There are people who have an over inflated sense of their own importance and have little or no regard for others that they come in contact with throughout their lives. These are the people who seem to be over confident and feel that they only deign to walk upon the earth, but in reality they will typically lack any confidence whatsoever. This display of egotism will often have the opposite effect on those around them and cause others to criticize them, but in effect, this criticism is exactly the opposite thing that a narcissist wants to hear and they can easily have their already low self-esteem shattered by any form of criticism.

What is a Narcissist?

The dictionary defines a narcissist as someone who finds themselves overly important, self-involved, vain, and selfish and that finds considerable amounts of satisfaction from admiring their own attributes. We have all seen examples of narcissistic behavior around us from the person who constantly has to talk about their own achievements, spends countless hours primping and admiring themselves in the mirror or constantly talks about themselves to no end causing other people to want to leave their company. The self-involved narcissist often displays no concern for other people and in all situations tries to bring the topic of conversation back around to themselves rather than including people around them.

So how do you tell if you, or someone that you know is a narcissist? One of the first considerations for a narcissist is that they typically will act as if the entire world revolves around them. They will typically be looking for compliments and praise that focuses just on themselves and may even downplay how others feel and their emotions. If they happen to disagree or if you say something that is not complimentary they will become withdrawn and cold and take a lot of time warming back up to the situation and engaging. Their ego will typically be very fragile despite the inflated image that they present and they can be very difficult to manage and unpleasant to be around.

Narcissist Description

While everyone can display narcissistic behavior from time to time, here are some symptoms to watch for if your behavior or someone around you is displaying more than just normal self-confidence. Many narcissists will have a very egocentric and inflated ego that will get in the way of their normal relationships. They may engage in activities with others, but will tend to always bring the situation back around so that it focuses on them and their best interests. They will constantly be looking for attention from others and have a desire to constantly be the center of attention in a group or a crowd. If they cannot be the center of attention they will become disproportionately unhappy and withdrawn, and maybe even start to act very childlike. Severe cases of narcissistic personality disorder can cause the sufferer to lash out at those around them until they again become the center of attention.

Narcissists typically have a difficult time forming meaningful relationships with other people because of their constant desire for attention. They will often attract others to them, but the relationships will be shallow and not meaningful as they are more concerned with themselves than the needs of others. They will be attracted to those who constantly praise them and build them up or place them on a pedestal. These relationships will lack any substance and people will finally grow tired of having to constantly praise the narcissist and will finally just leave or abandon them altogether. Worse yet, when someone with a lack of self-esteem latches on to a narcissist they will constantly live in the shadow of the narcissist. They define their own sense of purpose based on what the narcissist is and will have no sense of self. It essentially becomes a codependent relationship where the insecure person and the narcissist feed off of each other.

Medical Considerations

Narcissistic personality disorder can be very difficult to treat. One of the primary reasons that people do not seek treatment is a result of the disease itself in that they do not think that they have a problem that requires treatment. They feel perfectly happy locked in their own little world with very few people around them unless they are there to feed their own ego.

The narcissistic personality disorder condition is displayed in people who have an inflated sense of their own importance and go through life constantly seeking out the attention and admiration of those around them. They lack all consideration for other people and will simply dismiss them as unimportant unless they are providing the admiration that people with this disorder crave. This disorder can cause problems in all areas of a person's life and will impact their ability to form long lasting relationships of any type with other humans.

The symptoms for narcissistic personality disorder include having a very exaggerated feeling of their own importance, wanting to be recognized as better than everyone else even if their accomplishments and actions do not warrant this recognition, overly inflating their own accomplishments or their capabilities, a tendency to fantasize about success or power, trying to find a trophy-mate for a relationship, only associating with other people who they feel are on their own level, shunning those they feel are below them, and displaying a constant sense of entitlement for everything around them.

Many people with this disorder will expect to always receive special favors when they associate with other people and will become overbearing with their sense of entitlement to these favors. They will often take advantage of others to make sure that they get what they feel they are entitled to receive. Narcissistic personality disorder will often make the sufferer feel that everyone around them envies them and wants to be like them and they will behave in a very haughty or even arrogant manner towards others around them. Someone suffering from this disorder may display all or some of these symptoms to varying degrees.

Treatment for this type of disorder will typically revolve around therapy and learning how to better deal with other people. There are no specific medical treatments or medications available that are used besides therapy, but if other secondary symptoms are present, such as depression or anxiety, these symptoms can be treated while working in therapy on the underlying issues for the narcissism.

Narcissism is more typically seen in men than in women and there is no biological cause that underlies this condition. Many guess that this condition begins with the parent-child relationship when parents will overly praise a child and their accomplishments. This can also be a side effect from a broken home when the parents split up and the child only spends certain portions of their time with each parent. As a result, the parents tend to lavish attention on the child trying to win their affection, creating a mutated sense of worth in the child.

When this happens, the child goes through life thinking they are much better than they are and this can continue into adulthood. While many children will receive attention and praise from their parents, only a low percentage will actually develop narcissistic personality disorder. There is no need to stop lavishing attention on a child for fear of developing this disorder; just continue to praise when needed and when it is truly deserved so that the child will understand praise and what they did to deserve that praise in a healthy and balanced manner.

Typical Behaviors

Narcissistic personality disorder is one of a broad range of disorders where people have a behavior pattern that falls well outside the norms of society. These behavior patterns will cause them to feel and act in ways that separate them from their peers and will often cause issues with their relationships, jobs, and overall ability to function within society. There are behaviors that we can look for when we are trying to identify if someone is a narcissist. For example, people suffering from this disorder will often try to turn the conversation towards themselves and their achievements; they will constantly monopolize the conversation and avoid talking about anyone beside himself or herself. Many times they will come across as conceited and pretentious or called a snob. They will distance themselves from other people who do not share their love of themselves and will struggle with even basic daily relationships.

When a narcissist does not get the attention that he/she believes they deserve, they will withdraw and become very antisocial or start to mope. They will often perceive even a compliment as criticism and will not be able to re-engage with other people once their low self-esteem takes over. They will withdraw and feel shame or highly vulnerable and will become closed off to other people as they "lick their wounds" and try to fix their wounded ego.

More severe cases of narcissism can cause the person to lash out at others and become violent, often demonstrating severe mood swings and other personality disorders which can require medical intervention to help them to find a cure.

Example of a Narcissist
There are many famous examples of narcissists throughout history who have used their affliction to stroke their own egos while they go about their work. One highly famous leader who suffered from numerous mental inflictions, including narcissistic personality disorder, was Adolf Hitler. Hitler became famous throughout the world for all the atrocities he committed during his time leading Germany into world domination during World War II and was notorious for having little regard for the feelings or desires of other people. Another famous narcissist who was alive during Hitler's era was Joseph Mengele who also suffered from multiple afflictions. His behavior showed a constant need for attention and power which he gained through killing innocent children during this horrendous and terrible time of our history. Joseph Stalin, too,

was preoccupied with power, vanity, and control so much so that he jailed anyone who did not agree with him.

Not all narcissists are evil rulers, however, there are more subtle examples of narcissism in society such as Alec Baldwin and Sharon Stone, two actors who both display these tendencies to constantly draw attention their way with no regard for the feelings of other people. There's Donald Trump, who would also be considered a narcissist who seems to constantly search out new ways to draw him attention, even establishing a television show where he is the center feature.

Eva Peron, the wife of the Argentinian ruler, was also a narcissist who drew attention her way and would become very down if she were not the center of attention. Recently, there is Simon Cowell, the British talk show host and celebrity columnist who constantly seeks out the spotlight to fill his desire to be the center of attention. Many stars are notably narcissistic and their own desire for attention is the reason that they are famous. These people spend their entire lives striving for the next big attention grabbing stunt from risky death-defying adventures to performing sex acts on video then sharing the videos on the internet.

There are a variety of other movie stars, TV stars and celebrities with a narcissistic tendency in their personality, but each one has this personality trait in a different degree. Some let it show overtly, while others are still able to maintain good relations with other people and keep their narcissistic tendencies under wraps. Some personalities were able to corral their tendencies like Margaret Thatcher and Joan Crawford and still be successful while others constantly drive people away with their obnoxious actions such as Kayne West or the Kardashians.

Strategies to be Effective (Family, Co-workers, Friends, Random Encounters)

When you are dealing with someone who has narcissistic personality disorder, one of the first things you want to encourage him or her to do is to seek medical help. The best medical help for this condition is psychotherapy to help learn how to better relate with others and how to develop meaningful relationships with those around you. Therapy will allow a narcissist to learn what is causing the emotions, such as distrust and loathing of others. They will also learn how to accept and keep personal relationships and learn how to better tolerate failure and criticism from others. Overall, therapy will provide the tools that narcissists need to be able to better function in society as a whole.

If a family member or friend suffers from narcissistic personality disorder, then there are some strategies to help you manage the issues that you might face. The first tip is to keep things on a practical level. When you keep things on a practical level you will look at simple goals and objectives to accomplish rather than focusing on the fact that you are dealing with and interacting with a narcissistic individual. The next step is to stay distant and to separate your own emotional needs from the person suffering from narcissism. A true narcissist will have no way to understand the emotional needs of others and as a result the needs a person exhibits will not be met. If you emotionally separate yourself from a person with this disorder and look to fill your needs with another person instead, you will be better able to better deal with and manage their behaviors. This is one situation where therapy for the members of the family can be very helpful in maintaining sanity within the relationship.

The next step within a family environment is to define some limits that you must stay within. These limits are exceptionally important in any discussion and you must maintain them to keep your sanity. This does not require that you communicate these limits to the person who is suffering from this disorder. In fact, it might be wise of you to just keep these to yourself to avoid any potential hostility.

Another tip when dealing with someone with narcissistic personality disorder is to avoid getting in a conflict with them. This type of person will habitually try and argue and these arguments could disintegrate into a confrontation that can only end badly. Under all situations avoid confrontation and try to resolve any issues through other means. You cannot reason with someone who is suffering from this disorder and if you try, you will only end up in an exercise in futility as you attempt to resolve your issues in a logical manner with someone who is illogical.

Trying to gain more understanding of their condition is another strategy that will help to resolve issues with someone suffering from this disorder. Take the time to read studies and discuss the latest research with doctors and therapists to gain a better understanding of what is driving the person to behave how they are. With knowledge is power so the more information that you can gather the better chance that you will at least understand their perspective and be better equipped to deal with their issues.

There is a theory that narcissistic parents can produce narcissistic children, but with early intervention these children can learn how to deal with a parent who is a narcissist. Sometimes with early intervention and assistance children can avoid becoming narcissistic themselves and both know how to manage the symptom and avoid assuming that role themselves.

When dealing with narcissists in any situation from family to co-workers, everyone must understand that the narcissists' mind categorizes people and how they should behave. If a person falls outside of their categorization this can cause unnecessary stress in the relationship and worry for the people involved. As a result, people must realize that the narcissist "marches to the beat of a different drummer" than a majority of the population and when they freak out because someone does not fall in the category that they placed the person into, they must accept the situation and move on. Acceptance, however, is not an easy thing for a narcissist to do, so people must instead accommodate them and help them to reposition their view on the person within their minds and thoughts for a better relationship.

Chapter 4: Tips for Managing a Relationship with Someone with Bipolar Disorder

Bipolar disorder, or manic-depressive disorder, is a condition that some people will suffer from that causes them to have varying mood swings many times throughout a day. These mood swings will cause them to be extremely happy and euphoric with masses of energy (mania) to experiencing severe depression. Sometimes people will feel these symptoms simultaneously which can severely disrupt a person's ability to exist throughout the day and work and co-exist with other people. When a person suffers from bipolar disorder they will have a very difficult time working and surviving with other people until they are able to seek treatment for their condition.

What is a Bipolar Disorder?

Bipolar disorder is a mental condition that many people face during their lives either because they develop the disorder themselves or someone in their family is a carrier of the condition. With bipolar disorder, there are biological changes within the brain of the person suffering from this condition including a chemical imbalance in the neurotransmitters that control how people feel. There also are hormonal differences present in some people who develop these symptoms. Some people that suffer from the effects of bipolar disorder will have a severe hormonal imbalance that will trigger episodes of the disease.

There are reports and studies that have shown that bipolar disorder runs in families and that if a parent suffers from the condition then a child is also at risk of suffering from the condition. Researchers are trying to find the genes or sets of genes that put people at risk for the disease and to help determine if it is truly an inherited disorder. Since it does run in families, if you have a parent or relative that suffers from the condition then you will want to be aware of the symptoms within your family so that if that person suffering from the disease begins to exhibit symptoms, you will be able to quickly address the issues and get help for the family member or even possibly yourself.

Stress can trigger bipolar disorder in someone that is predisposed to the condition. If there is stress, abuse, a traumatic event, or a significant loss, the person can be prone to developing symptoms of the condition as well. It all comes down to monitoring their moods and watching for any of the key symptoms that are involved with bipolar disorder to get treatment and address the situation early on.

Bipolar Description
Bipolar disorder is broken into three different categories in order to fully understand the

disorder and what is going on when people suffer from this condition. First is Bipolar I, which causes the basic mood swings from euphoria to severe depression. Bipolar I symptoms will range from mild to very severe and sometimes can be dangerous to the person and those around them. These episodes will impact their day-to-day lives and cause them to have problems in school, work, and in their relationships. This is the most severe case of bipolar disorder.

Bipolar II has similar symptoms as Bipolar I, but will have more mild mood swings and less violent symptoms that can still permit the person to have a relatively normal life and still go to school and maintain a job. The mood swings seen in Bipolar II will typically last longer, but be less severe or less manic than Bipolar I.

The mildest form of bipolar disorder is called cyclothymic disorder and people with these symptoms will still have the hypomania and depression symptoms that the other types of bipolar disorder will experience, but their symptoms are the least severe of all three types.

Within all three types, people can experience a mixed episode of bipolar disorder where they experience both euphoria and depression at the same time. Imagine the conflicted emotions that someone experiencing both symptoms of the condition must feel and how they can struggle to get by when facing these issues!

Medical Considerations

To be medically diagnosed as having bipolar disorder, the person must meet the criteria spelled out in the Diagnostic and Statistical Manual of Mental Disorders that is published by the American Psychiatric Association. This guideline provides assistance to doctors and psychiatrists in diagnosing the symptoms and finding help for people suffering from this condition. The criteria for bipolar disorder includes the following:

In order to meet the criteria for a manic episode the person must have a clearly defined period lasting a week or more that includes symptoms such as inflated self-esteem, feelings of grandiosity, demonstrate a decreased need to sleep, be unusually talkative, having racing thoughts, be easily distracted, show less goal-orientation such as losing the drive to follow through with work or school, demonstrating behaviors that could have a risky outcome such as shopping sprees, foolish business investments, or taking risky sexual partners.

All of these symptoms, in combination with the manic episode that is severe enough to impact their performance in their everyday life, will be used to consider a diagnosis. A hypomanic episode will last for at least four days and have similar symptoms as a manic episode and a major depressive episode can exhibit these symptoms over several weeks.

The symptoms that either the person, or those around them, must watch out for include being in a depressed or even tearful mood throughout the day, showing diminished interest in daily activities especially those things that used to bring pleasure to the person, demonstrating significant weight loss even if they have not been dieting or exercising, and experiencing insomnia or increased napping and wanting to sleep during the day. Fatigue and lack of energy may be seen almost constantly and they will have little motivation to do anything or get anything done. They will be indecisive almost constantly and they could also have thoughts of suicide.

Once the criteria they meet has been determined, then doctors will begin to determine the correct treatment path to help the person get back on track to be functional during the day and in their lives, jobs, and relationships.

Aggressive and often lifelong treatment is required for people who suffer from bipolar disorder and will include a combination of medication and therapy both individually and with a family group if applicable. Some patients who are diagnosed with severe symptoms may require hospitalization if they are suicidal or a danger to themselves or those around them or if they become psychotic and detached from reality.

Doctors will typically prescribe drugs immediately to help bring the mood swings under control right away and will continue this treatment throughout the patient's life. Patients who are on medication to control their moods cannot stop taking this medication or they risk the symptoms coming back and this can initiate a full blown manic-depressive episode. People who take mood controlling drugs should not drink alcohol because this can negatively impact the bipolar disorder treatment and make it difficult to control and treat.

People with bipolar disorder will also require therapy in order to better control, treat, and manage the disorder in their day-to-day lives. Doctors and psychiatrists will use a combination of cognitive behavioral therapy and psycho education therapy to help the person suffering from the disorder and their families to deal with the condition and manage it on a daily basis. Cognitive therapy will help people to learn to identify the triggers that cause an episode to occur and to cope with or avoid those situations so that they do not have an episode.

Psycho education therapy for a family will help loved ones to understand the signs and to stop an episode before it becomes an issue for the loved one and to better understand the condition and what their loved one is going through with this condition. Family support for this condition is critical to helping a loved one survive and receive the support they urgently need to get better or control their symptoms.

Typical Behaviors

When someone is dealing with bipolar disorder, their lives will be consumed by the highs and lows of the condition. When they are going through a depressive episode they will display an extremely depressed mood and that could even become tearful. They will show very little interest in the world around them, even about things that used to bring them considerable joy and happiness. They will stop playing sports or taking part in other hobbies and pastimes that they used to enjoy. They may experience a little or sometimes extreme weight loss, have difficulty sleeping, seem constantly agitated and have overall fatigue throughout their body. They will act guilty or show feelings of worthlessness and may have trouble making decisions. Some people will even go so far as to think about death or suicide and will struggle with even the simplest activities like getting out of bed or getting dressed.

A manic, or euphoric, episode will cause people to experience an unusual elevated mood and will be the exact opposite of the depressive state of the condition. They will be very optimistic and excited, they will have loads of energy and can go days without sleeping. They may have erratic behavior and this behavior may demonstrate unsafe practices or be very risky. They may act all powerful and become suddenly very driven at work. Their behaviors may make them more talkative and very easily distracted throughout the day. People and family members will find it very difficult to be around them as they exude energy and jump from activity to activity, not stopping to take any breaks. When people are in this phase of bipolar mania they can become agitated as well.

Example of Bipolar Disorder
There are many famous people who have shared their condition with the public as they struggle to overcome this disease and it is estimated that throughout the United States there are 5.7 million people who suffer from different levels of this condition. Many celebrities and actors were diagnosed with this condition and demonstrated the unusual lows and highs that came from this diagnosis.

One famous celebrity who announced that she was struggling with this disease was Carrie Fisher who initially denied that she had this problem, attributing it to alcohol addiction, but once she finally got treated was able to turn her life around and become a successful author in addition to her acting fame from the Star Wars movies. Another famous actor who struggled with bipolar disorder is Jean-Claude Van Damme, a popular action movie star, who had his life unravel as the symptoms took over his life, but finally he stabilized with treatment and help.

Linda Hamilton, another famous star who claims fame from the Terminator series of movies, also suffers from bipolar disorder. She now is on medication and better able to manage the highs and lows that come along with this condition. Even the famous Irish singer Sinead O'Connor has been diagnosed with bipolar disorder and finally got her life back in order with treatment and therapy. A more recent superstar to speak out about her bipolarity and her desire to educate everyone on mental illness is Demi Lovato. Demi is a songwriter, singer, and actress who has been very forthcoming of her struggles and fight to get her life back in control through therapy and medication; she is an example of how people with bipolar disorder can still live a "normal" life even with the disorder.

Strategies to be Effective (Family, Co-workers, Friends, Random Encounters)

Maintaining and keeping healthy relationships is one of the biggest issues that people suffering from bipolar disorder face in their everyday lives. Many will have issues with their spouses and divorce is very common in these situations. People with bipolar disorder will have difficulty holding down a job and can become very depressed with their symptoms since they can be so severe.

The first step for families to manage a family member with this condition is to seek professional, medical help. People with bipolar disorder need treatment to help them balance their lives and to get back on track. Medication and therapy combined will help to bring them back in line for a healthy life and relationships with others. They need to get regular sleep and have good meals and exercise. They need to establish a healthy routine and way of life to give them the sound basis they will need to successfully treat their condition.

When dealing with friends and co-workers who demonstrate the signs of this condition, first and foremost you will want to understand their condition. Due to this condition, they are often not able to control their day-to-day lives and feelings and will have a difficult time functioning in the work environment. Encourage them to seek help to get their lives back in order, but most of all do not judge. They may feel that they have things under control or may be in the initial phases of treatment and pointing out where they are failing could trigger an episode.

When a person is undergoing treatment for bipolar disorder they will be focusing on identifying the triggers that cause them to have an episode. They will then receive therapy and support for these issues and advice and strategies to avoid these situations where they can trigger an episode and slip back into a manic or depressive state. People will often struggle for quite some time before they manage to get their symptoms entirely under control so it is very important for them to be in a supportive environment that will help them to become contributing members of society again.

Chapter 5: Tips for Managing a Relationship with Someone who has Multiple Personalities

Multiple personality disorder falls under the umbrella of dissociate disorders where people will have a lack of continuity between thoughts, memories, and actions that impacts their identity as a person. Sometimes people suffering from this disorder will have amnesia and not remember who they are from one day to another and in other cases they may take on a completely different persona altogether. No matter how the symptoms of multiple persona manifest themselves, treatment is critical to help the person cope and to reintegrate back into society and their family as a whole.

What is a Multiple Personalities Disorder?

Multiple personality disorder is a type of dissociative disorder where people will disconnect from reality and will not be able to link memories with their daily lives and interactions with other people. They will have issues with identity and may demonstrate a completely different persona with their actions and reactions to events being unpredictable and completely opposite to the person that others knew them as. People suffering from this condition are often unable to engage in society or hold a job; there is always the risk that one of the other personalities could show up at the work place making it an uncomfortable situation. The goal for someone suffering from multiple personality disorder is to regain control of their lives through therapy and treatment so that they can rejoin society with the tools they need to be successful.

Multiple Personalities Description
When people have multiple personality disorder they will display the several signs and symptoms of this condition. They will have complete memory loss of certain people or time events or amnesia of certain events. They will often have other mental health conditions that go along with this disorder such as depression, anxiety, and suicidal thoughts or attempts at suicide. They will feel like they are detached from themselves and the world around them and feel like they are walking around in a bubble without being able to interact with the world around them. People with this condition will have a blurred sense of their own identify and have difficulty relating to other human beings on any level, causing problems when people are trying to keep a job or have a relationship with someone.

As the name of the disorder suggests, people suffering from multiple personality disorder will often demonstrate completely different personas.

These personas will have a unique way of acting, facial expressions, accents and even a different language, which has been reported in some cases. It can be amazing to observe someone suffering from this condition and see them switch personalities because it is as if you did not know it was the same person you would suspect that someone entirely new had just arrived and taken over your friend or family member's body. It is a modern day version of invasion of the body snatchers!

Because this condition is so severe, until people can get their symptoms under control they need to be under supervision and monitored to protect themselves from harm. Friends or family members can help out in these times to protect their loved one while they seek help and treatment.

Medical Considerations
There are three medical considerations for people who are suffering from multiple personality disorder to be diagnosed with the condition. The first symptom that doctors and psychiatrists will watch for is dissociative amnesia. This type of amnesia is more severe than just everyday forgetfulness where people can forget if they locked the door or turned off the coffee pot. This type of forgetfulness has no medical condition or injury associated with it

and will cause a complete loss of memory about themselves and their personality.

People with dissociative amnesia have been found wandering around in a dissociative fugue with episodes lasting from minutes to years. They will have no recollection of who they are or what they were doing when the attack occurred. This type of amnesia will cause the person to completely forget who they are and anything about their history and how they came to be where they are at. They will be unable to recall events, family or people they may have known their entire life or they may forget events surrounding just one particular phase or time period in their life.

The next symptom that doctors and psychiatrists will look for is dissociative identity disorder. This is demonstrated when a person literally switches to a new identity and that new identity causes new behaviors and facial expressions to take over the person and their body, this is where the "body snatchers" come in. People can demonstrate one or more personalities and they may even have different names for each personality. People suffering from this disorder report that they feel they have multiple voices within their heads and it feels like there are many people talking and living inside of them. Each time one of these personalities emerges it will have a different history, mannerisms and sometimes may even require the wearing of glasses. The changes between personalities is noticeable and each personality may have some or varying degrees of knowledge of the other personalities.

Finally, the third symptom that doctors and psychiatrists will be looking for when making a diagnosis is depersonalization and derealization disorder. This condition involves an ongoing feeling that the person is detached from their self and watching their life unfold around them like a movie. They may feel like they are in a dreamlike state and this condition can go on for just a few moments or last for many years. This is different than a feeling of shock, which a person experiences due to a traumatic event, instead this is a long-standing feeling that they have been jerked from the world and are watching events unfold as if they were looking through a window.

All of the described symptoms will be used to make a diagnosis of multiple personality disorder and will guide doctors and psychiatrists to identifying the correct treatment and therapy to help a person cope with their disorder and get back to living their life.

There are known causes that have led to people developing multiple personality disorder. It is believed that this condition is a result of severe trauma or stress when a person was younger.

This could include a long history of sexual or emotional abuse or an extremely traumatic event that made the home environment a frightening place for a child to grow up. These dissociative disorders will develop as a coping mechanism by the child which can lead to issues later on in life when the child grows up and goes into adulthood.

The reason that these personalities form during the childhood years is that during this time, a child is still developing this sense of personal identity. When a tragic event happens during this time frame, the child tries to cope in the best way they can which can cause them to develop alternate personalities. These coping mechanisms will then extend into their adult lives and these conditions will surface, possibly as multiple personality disorder. Consider the famous horror fiction story The Shining written by Stephen King. In this popular story (and Hollywood movie), the child star within the story developed multiple personalities that drove him throughout the movie. The story, and movie, describes how difficult times in his childhood home have allowed this issue to pop up in the child who is just a victim of his environment. Mr. King was very thorough in his book showing the negative impact a poor childhood environment can have on people when they are in their formative years.

Unfortunately, for people suffering from multiple personality disorder there is no known drug therapy that will help to eliminate this condition. The only treatment that they currently have available is therapy. During therapy, counselors and psychosocial therapists will help provide strategies for the person to use to cope with this condition. They will give them tips for managing relationships and help becoming integrated back into society.

Typical Behaviors
Many years ago, there was a short story written by the famous author Ray Bradbury in which he described a world where multiple personalities were the norm and all people exhibited these different personalities on a set schedule and with each switch they had different homes, families, and wore different makeup to distinguish them from their alternate persona. People who did not have distinctly two different personalities were considered abnormal, were committed, and treated to try to bring the two distinct personalities out in these people. People suffering from multiple personality disorder can have very distinct and different personalities just like what was described in this story. When someone switches personalities, the change is so complete you may not recognize the person at all.

Have you ever walked down the street and seen someone across from you and swore it was a friend only to walk over and take a closer look and realize that something is off in their appearance and it wasn't them? When someone close to you goes through an episode of multiple personalities it is similar to seeing someone you think you recognize on the street. Their outward features are completely the same, but their actions, expressions, and behaviors are completely different than you are accustomed to making it very difficult to be with the person when they are not the person that you know.

Another behavior that people with multiple personality disorder will demonstrate is when they disconnect from reality. They may go through the motions of their day, but they will be completely disengaged from what they are doing. It will seem like they are physically present, but they are not able to engage in life and what they are doing.

Example of Multiple Personalities
There are examples of famous people who have been diagnosed with multiple personality disorder and managed to overcome their obstacles and be successful despite their condition. For example, Adam Duritz, a famous songwriter who was the lead singer for the group "Counting Crows" was diagnosed with dissociative identity disorder. The condition

negatively impacted his relationship with his girlfriend and family until he found a strategy to manage the condition and move on with his life. Another famous author, Truddi Chase, was also diagnosed with this condition. She suffered from dissociative identity disorder as a result of a childhood full of physical and sexual abuse and had a hard time coping until he was diagnosed.

The famous model Marilyn Monroe also suffered from dissociative identity disorder and it was said that her grandparents also suffered from this condition. She attempted to treat the condition, but unfortunately, despite her success in life was not successful in treatment and passed away due to a prescription drug overdose. The experience that Marilyn Monroe had with this condition highlights how important it is to seek knowledgeable help for treatment and not try to manage it yourself, especially with drugs and alcohol.

Another famous personality who suffered through a public break down is the singer Britney Spears. This singer showed signs and symptoms of dissociative identity disorder shortly after she divorced Kevin Federline. She had a very noticeable breakdown where she was caught in public shaving her head and acting very erratically. Her family stepped in to help get treatment for her and to get control of her life and her career though after her public breakdown, she has not successfully recreated her image as a top tier singer.

Finally, the famous mixed martial artist and football player, Hershel Walker, was also diagnosed with this disorder. When he went public and discussed his issues with the disorder, one of his most notable comments was that he did not remember winning the Heisman Trophy. This significant accomplishment was completely forgotten because of his dissociative identity disorder issue that was not yet diagnosed. This demonstrates just how significant this disorder actually is and how it disrupts the lives and the careers of the people who suffer from this condition. Without treatment and help he may never have realized what he was able to accomplish in life, but with treatment he is now functioning more normally within society and can better understand his great achievements.

Strategies to be Effective (Family, Co-workers, Friends, Random Encounters)

When a family member or close friend is diagnosed with multiple personality disorder the first thing that everyone must remember is to not take it personally. There is nothing that you have done to initiate this condition and it does not mean that the person that you knew does not still exist and love you in return. Without the help, love, and understanding of a strong family many people will lose their loved ones due to exhibiting multiple personalities, sometimes which do not acknowledge or remember people within their own family. Children and spouses can feel rejected almost as if there was a death in the family when the person that they know and love no longer recognizes them or returns their feelings. This disorder can break apart families very easily and cause considerable heartache, but there are strategies that people can take to cope with these issues. Numerous divorces and broken families have resulted because of this condition.

Therapy and coping strategies are available for the family and friends of someone suffering from multiple personality disorder. Doctors and psychiatrists will provide tools and strategies to manage the relationships and help these sufferers to develop a semblance of a normal life. The symptoms will never completely go away and people will have to deal with each one as they come up, however. Some people have found that grief counseling also helps to overcome the initial shock of this diagnosis and lets them move forward and assist their loved one with treatment.

Friends and co-workers who suffer from this condition will also occasionally need to offer their support. If they go through an episode of severe amnesia they could lose all memory of who they are, where they live, or even where they are. These feelings could cause them to panic, without a friendly and understanding person around to help them to get them help. If someone has an episode while you are present, it is important to keep calm and first and foremost make sure that they do not hurt themselves. Gently guide them back to somewhere safe and help them to work through the episode until you can notify a close family member or friend to help take care of them.

Chapter 6: Tips for Managing a Relationship with Someone who is Neurotic

Just about everyone we know will have some type of neurotic behavior that they demonstrate. These behaviors will range from being just a minor inconvenience to a debilitating and annoying action, but they can negatively impact the people around us and can cause issues in our day-to-day relationship as we try to manage our interactions with other people. No matter how big or small our neurotic actions are, if you understand the underlying causes and conditions you can better develop strategies to deal with the people who are suffering from these conditions in their daily lives.

What is Neurotic?

The dictionary describes neurotic as the functional disorder where a person demonstrates feelings of anxiety and obsessional thoughts that cause compulsive acts when they do not demonstrate symptoms of any disease or condition. This is a relatively mild form of a personality disorder which is actually quite common within the population and often written off as a personality quirk or unusual trait.

Neuroses Description

People who suffer from neuroses or have neurotic traits will often have a negative emotional state and feel very down and depressed. They will experience guilt, anger and envy much more frequently than the average individual which can drive them into a neurotic state of mind. They will be very sensitive to stress and have a difficult time coping with day to day stress in their lives that people without this condition can often manage without any significant issues. They will be very prone to despair and get highly frustrated over seemingly small and insignificant issues.

People suffering from neuroses will often be shy and very self-conscious about themselves and their actions. They will be ashamed of their behavior and try not to draw unnecessary attention to themselves. Their condition is difficult to recognize because it may seem like a personality issue, but they do not have any hallucinations or delusions and their behaviors stay within the socially acceptable norms.

People will range from low to high on their emotional stability when it comes to being neurotic. People who are on the low scale will seem calm and even tempered and rarely show big outbursts of emotion or anger. Those who rank high on the neurotic scale can frequently display anger and be very emotional and difficult to manage.

Medical Considerations

The medical community does not use the terms neurosis or neuroticism in their diagnostic vernacular as commonly as they did in the past. Now the symptoms and issues that patients face are clumped under different disorders such as anxiety or depression based on the symptoms that they display.

In the past, the medical definition for neurosis included an overall emotional instability that does not interfere with the person's ability to function within society. They may be under extreme stress, but can still function and get by in life. For example, consider a person who was bitten by a dog when they were younger; later in life they may become anxious around dogs or fearful whenever they encounter another dog. When a person experiences some type of neurotic behavior it is often based on past experiences and there will be some basis to their fear even if that fear is unfounded in the current situation.

There is no specific treatment for neuroses since it does not typically interfere with a person's day to day life. It is only when the behaviors become debilitating that a person will seek help for their condition and require medical intervention and therapy.

Typical Behaviors

Consider the example of the person who developed a fear of dogs. When they were younger they were bitten by a dog and went through a traumatic experience with this type of animal. As a result, all future interactions with dogs were impacted and the person became fearful of all dogs as a result of the actions of one dog in their past. It doesn't matter that other dogs do not cause them harm, their opinion of all dogs is now skewed by the one interaction that they had with that one animal.

Neurotic behavior can stem from a variety of traumatic events that will make a person fearful of experiencing that behavior again. For someone who had a traumatic childhood, they could have an unusual reaction to yelling or argumentative behaviors. If someone was in an airplane crash or accident, they could develop a fear of flying; the same for someone who was thrown from a horse could develop a fear of horseback riding. The key to each of these neuroses is some type of traumatic event that happened earlier in life that caused the person to develop an irrational fear of that activity in the future.

When someone is experiencing a neurosis, they could demonstrate a wide range of behaviors. They could just say they prefer not to be in that situation or they could experience debilitating fear causing them to be unable to move.

Example of Neurotic Behavior
I heard the story of a friend who was an avid horseback rider who had been working with horses her entire life. One day she had an unfortunate accident and was thrown from a horse, causing considerable damage and injury. When she was able to return to the barn she found she could successfully interact with horses, but when she went to get on one she began to shake uncontrollably and became extremely frightened. The horse sensed her fear and began to prance and get very agitated. She ended up going to work with a trainer to overcome her new fear of riding so that she could once again enjoy the sport that she loved so much. This shows how a traumatic event can cause a neurotic behavior, but with treatment, the neurosis can be overcome and someone can work through the issue that they are having.

Another example of neurotic behavior is a new parent. New parents read countless books and articles about the numerous conditions and potential problems their child will/could face as they grow up. The new parents will try and put a bubble around their child to protect them from all the dangers of the environment and keep them safe. Their behavior becomes neurotic when they begin to child proof the home of family members and friends before they visit or refusing to visit the homes of families who do not have children for fear that their child could be harmed. This over-protective neurosis can continue throughout the life of the child and cause the child to lead an overly protected life and have very few experiences of its own. Often this sheltered child will need to learn certain skills later in life that they should have learned when they were younger, but they were hampered by their parent's neuroses.

Strategies to be Effective (Family, Co-workers, Friends, Random Encounters)

Managing neuroses in friends, families, and with co-workers can be challenging, but with a little accommodation it is not too significant. Communication is key so that you will not place a person in a situation where they are forced to address their neurosis head on and become debilitated.

For example, I remember the example of a co-worker who was deathly afraid of flying and would not get on an airplane to save their life. To accommodate his neurosis, the employer allowed him to travel by train when he was required to travel. Each one on the team helped to accommodate his issues and a trip that should have taken four hours to visit a customer site instead took four days. By knowing these issues in advance, the team was able to accommodate and work around their teammate's fears while still being effective.

Another example of how to accommodate neurotic behavior was seen when my family came to visit. I have four dogs in my home that are very friendly and well socialized, but when people come to visit I am often forced to accommodate their fears of my canine family by locking them away in another room. This has caused issues with these family members not wanting to visit because of these fears. Many dog owners face this same issue and refuse to lock away the canines, choosing them over family members.

Finally, I've seen examples of neurotic behaviors when driving in a vehicle; this behavior is one that I regularly experience, but have learned to accommodate. As a young driver, I was rear-ended while at a standstill making a left hand turn. The driver was easily going over 55 mph and the resulting accident put me in the hospital with severe pain and injuries. After I was released, every time I applied the brakes on my vehicle I would look into the rear view mirror for someone who had not stopped or noticed my brake lights. This neurosis actually prevented several additional accidents when the person behind me did not stop, but became an annoying habit when I exhibited the same behavior as the passenger in the vehicle.

Everyone that we encounter will have some degree of neurotic behavior and it is always better to just accommodate the behavior and be understanding of the person and their issues rather than try to change the person's behavior. Most of the time there is a traumatic event in their past that has helped them to form this neuroses and they have put self-preservation techniques in place to help them manage the rest of their lives and avoid a repeat of that traumatic situation.

Chapter 7: Tips for Managing a Relationship with a Hypochondriac

After a grueling day of taking four final examinations and intense studying the night before a college student is left with an intense headache. Instead of associating this headache with the pressure of taking four consecutive final examinations in a row and the cramming of information and studying the night before in the wee hours of the night, the exhausted student immediately jumps to the conclusion that the headache indicates that he is suffering from a tumor or possibly has had an aneurysm.

Hypochondriacs are a group of people who become overly obsessed with their health and believe that they have a/many life threatening condition(s). They will experience considerable anxiety when they hear about a new disease and may spend hours in the doctor's office requesting unnecessary tests when they actually are fine. This is typically a life-long condition that people and their families will have to manage, but with a few tips and some therapy there are strategies to make life with a hypochondriac more manageable. It can be as simple as a person having a slight cold and jumping to the conclusion that they have pneumonia or even the Ebola virus or include a more serious condition that debilitates people making them afraid to travel more than two blocks from their doctor's office for fear of contracting a deadly disease.

What is a Hypochondriac?

The dictionary definition of a hypochondriac is a person who becomes abnormally anxious and worried that they have some type of health condition that may or may not be life-threatening. They will hear about a condition or a disease from a movie, the television, or even read about it on the Internet and will become convinced that they have this condition. A hypochondriac will often visit a doctor numerous times and not be convinced when the doctor does not find any issues and they will continue on for a second opinion. They may spend hours in the doctor's office undergoing unnecessary tests and exams and still not be convinced that they are alright, no matter how many doctors tell them otherwise.

The medical community is not sure why some people develop this issue and take it to such an extreme. Some cases start when a loved one or family member passes away from a disease and the survivors become hyper vigilant for the same condition. Others who have this condition may be prone to it because of inherited traits or other life experiences. No matter which combination of events or factors combined to bring on this condition the person who is the hypochondriac can experience severe episodes of panic and obsessive compulsive disorder when they have convinced themselves that they have the medical condition.

Hypochondriac Description

The symptoms of a hypochondriac versus someone who has a normal worry about their health are what distinguish a hypochondriac from normal people. A hypochondriac will have long-term fears that they have a condition where a normal person will stop worrying once the doctor runs tests and tells them that they are all right. Hypochondriacs will think that every minor symptom and ache is the sign of something serious whereas a normal person can accept these minor issues as a part of life and not worry excessively. Someone who is a hypochondriac will constantly request additional tests, seek out second and third opinions and always believe that something is wrong whereas a normal person can accept the diagnosis and will seek a second opinion only when it is truly warranted.

Hypochondriacs will constantly talk about their symptoms with family, friends, and co-workers and will often be so obsessed with their potential illnesses that they do not talk about anything else. They will constantly perform self-examinations on an almost daily basis searching for issues and other symptoms. They will monitor their vital signs and begin to panic when they are even slightly different, versus a normal person who will not be obsessed with this constant monitoring of their health and issues.

When a hypochondriac reads about an illness or hears something new, he/she will almost instantly begin to attribute each of these symptoms applies to them even when there is nothing seriously wrong. If any of these descriptions applies to you or your loved one, then you may have a serious issue that needs to be addressed and you may want to get help.

Medical Considerations
When a doctor routinely sees a patient for numerous issues or suspected illnesses that turn out to be unfounded, they may begin to suspect that a patient is suffering from hypochondria. They will start to form this diagnosis by asking the patient to fill out a questionnaire that looks at their psychological conditions. Additionally, they will perform a physical exam looking for any issues or signs of disease. During the exam, they will check weight, vital signs, and listen to the heart and lungs to look for any issues. They may also check glands for swelling or look at any bumps. They may complete bloodwork and look for any abnormalities as well to rule out any medical condition. If everything checks out fine then they may begin to consider that the person may actually have a hypochondriac condition.

A full psychological exam will be conducted on the person to begin to understand what is going on in their lives and why they have begun to suspect they have a variety of conditions. A doctor or psychiatrist will discuss the symptoms with the person and help them to explain what is going on and why they think that they are sick. They will look at whether their thoughts are impacting their effectiveness in their day to day lives and will try and identify solutions that will help ease their concerns.

There is no set treatment for a hypochondriac besides the constant barrage of negative diagnosis and tests, which are not actually treatment, but a panacea to keep their worries at bay. They can seek counseling to help them cope with their symptoms on a day-to-day basis, but there are no drugs that can be taken to directly help with the hypochondriac type behaviors. When the symptoms become so severe that it causes secondary conditions such as depression or anxiety, these symptoms can be treated with medication that can help the patient to function again in life.

Typical Behaviors
It may be hard to believe, but every one of us has hypochondriac-type feelings. We are all naturally concerned about our health and if something appears out of the ordinary then it is only right that we should be concerned about it.

It is when these concerns and feelings begin to dominate our daily lives and conversations that we need to be concerned.

I remember the example of my grandparents who regularly told us about the new ailment that they were suffering from which just happened to be that week's feature in the newspaper. Each week in the medical section of the newspaper would feature a doctor who would write an article about a medical condition that elderly people should watch out for and each week we would hear a vivid description of how my grandparents had this exact condition. It did not help the situation that they did in fact have one of the conditions listed, but it was so common we were not surprised. Since they had one, they assumed they had all conditions and we were left hearing about the ailment of the week.

My friends in medical school while I was in college reported a similar phenomenon. As they learned about a new disease or condition, each one in the class would often report that they had the symptoms that were being described. I often laughed as one person was convinced they had dengue fever, even though they had never left the country, and the other reported they were convinced they had an exotic blood condition. Maybe their vulnerability was increased by the long hours they spent studying, but it was amusing to hear about their behaviors.

Fortunately, time did not permit them to constantly visit the doctor's office for tests and their heads were soon filled with a new disease or symptom that they were convinced that they had.

A true hypochondriac is not someone who just occasionally worries about their health, but instead they are constantly obsessing about their well-being. The topic of their health will become the focus of their lives and they are unable to do anything else. They will constantly discuss their issues with family, friends and co-workers and make numerous trips to the doctor's office for checkups or request tests and diagnostic procedures.

When family and friends start to avoid the uncomfortable conversations, hypochondriacs will even approach salespeople and strangers to go over all their symptoms and feed their worrisome behaviors by discussing all the problems they think that they have. They will have test after test done to find some problem and may become frustrated to realize that they are in fact healthy. When their behaviors cross the line from a normal worry to this type of psychotic neurosis, then it is time for them to seek help.

Example of a Hypochondriac
Many people throughout history have been notable hypochondriacs from famous world

leaders to scientists and even actors. Each person that had issues with hypochondria were able to manage and deal with their issues while still being successful in life.

Consider Charles Darwin, the developer of the scientific theory of evolution, who also happened to be a notorious hypochondriac. Despite all his knowledge, he was a neurotic hypochondriac who constantly looked for different cures to the ailments that he thought that he had. He kept a variety of records about his body and health even going so far as to keep records on his own flatulence.

A famous young actress, Abigail Breslin, also suffered from this condition. This young child actor prodigy was so concerned about her health and worried constantly that something was wrong, that she constantly would visit doctors. She would say she was sick and think something was wrong, but when asked to describe her symptoms she would just say that she did not have any. She would wear shoes at all times, even in bed, to avoid stepping on glass and refused to watch doctor shows on television for fear that she would find another condition that she would start obsessing about. Despite her issues, she went from a famous child actress and grew up to be a successful young adult with a stable acting career. She constantly worked to keep her symptoms from interfering with her career.

Adolf Hitler again gives us an example of someone who suffers from hypochondria. In addition to all his other mental conditions, this infamous leader was also a known hypochondriac and he fixated on his health. In fact, he did more than just fixate on his health; he would force doctors to prescribe numerous medicines for his real and imagined conditions. He did not travel anywhere without a doctor whom he would order to prescribe and treat him with a variety of medications even if the doctor did not feel the medication was warranted.

The author Hans Christian Anderson was also a noted hypochondriac who still went on to lead a relatively normal and successful life. He would constantly exaggerate the importance of small symptoms saying a spot on his face was going to cover his entire face or if he ate meat he would swallow a pin. These unfounded fears might have contributed to his success as a story teller.

Another example of a famous hypochondriac is the artist Andy Warhol. This highly successful artist was actually a very severe hypochondriac and would keep detailed notes on any sickness or issue that he faced. Despite his condition, however, he refused to go to the hospital for a legitimate illness, which may have expedited his death due to issues with a gall bladder.

Strategies to be Effective (Family, Co-workers, Friends, Random Encounters)

If you are one of the random people that are approached in a store or shopping mall by a hypochondriac then it is easy to dismiss them quickly. Unless you are truly interested in their medical discussion, it is perfectly polite to leave the conversation and them to their own worries. But friends, family, and co-workers cannot dismiss the situation quite as quickly as a random stranger. It is important to show concern for people and realize that no amount of convincing is going to help change their minds.

Hypochondriacs cannot be reasoned with, plain and simple. You must allow them their issues and then after an accommodating amount of listening try to redirect their focus maybe to a grandchild, pet, or favorite activity so that you will not have to listen to their next potential illness. It can be difficult to refocus their attention, but it is possible and you will find that they can be interesting to talk to when they are not discussing an illness. Some people look for some type of illness to seek attention and pity from the people around them. When you focus on the positive things in their life you will help them to see that they do not have to be sick to receive love and attention and this may help to diminish their need to focus on an illness and disease.

Chapter 8: Tips for Managing a Relationship with Someone who has Post Traumatic Stress Disorder (PTSD)

Post Traumatic Stress Disorder or PTSD began to come to the forefront with the most recent return of soldiers from assignments overseas. Without adequate support and assistance for their integration back into society upon their return, there have been many instances where they have committed crimes or suicide when they could not successfully assimilate back into society. These individuals faced a traumatic experience that their minds could not fully comprehend and it permanently skewed how they perceived and interacted with society as a whole. Their entire persona is impacted and all areas of their lives are permanently changed as they try to manage the seriousness of the mental issues that they are facing.

What is PTSD?

PTSD is an actual mental condition that can be triggered by a terrifying event. This could happen to anyone at any point in their life and is not solely attributed to soldiers who return from war. PTSD can be caused by a loss of a loved one, a serious accident, an attack, rape, or any other severely traumatic event. A person's mind will often struggle to come to terms with the event and will start to relive the event in their daily life. They may experience flashbacks and anxiety or could have very vivid nightmares when they try to sleep. They will have difficulty adjusting back to normal life and may be constantly prone to flashbacks. Symptoms can last for many years and even with treatment it can take a long time to get over the issues associated with this condition.

PTSD Description

There is no specific time frame for when PTSD can occur after someone has been involved in a traumatic event. Some have reported symptoms beginning within three months of the event while others have said the events took longer to show up, sometimes as long as years. The symptoms will often start to impact a person's day to day life and their relationships with others making it difficult for them to hold a job or maintain a stable relationship.

PTSD does not have to involve fighting on the front lines of a war or losing a loved one. Everyone has a different level of sensitivity and depending on the person, the definition of a 'significant or traumatic' event will vary. For some, this could be getting fired from a job, especially if it was during the holidays or with some extenuating circumstances. Others could see an accident or injury as a traumatic event and have issues after the event coping with the resulting stress. The most important consideration is to realize that each person will react and develop PTSD symptoms differently than another. Some people return from war zones and have no mental issues and quickly join back into society and can be successful with their families and relationships.

Medical Considerations
The symptoms of PTSD are grouped into four areas when someone is being diagnosed with this condition. The first area is whether they experience intrusive memories. This type of memory will happen frequently and often and will bring up the distressing issues surrounding the traumatic event. These memories will be vivid flashbacks and the victim will feel like they are reliving the event all over. They will often have very upsetting dreams of the event and these dreams will cause them to lose sleep and constantly relive the event that caused the problems. Severe emotional stress can trigger the flashbacks and can cause the sufferer to relive the traumatic event even if they are unrelated to what is happening to them currently. For example, if someone loses a beloved pet, the extreme emotional stress could trigger a PTSD flashback to another event.

The next symptom that doctors will look for is avoidance. When someone refuses to talk about the traumatic event or share the details then they are avoiding. Proper coping with a traumatic issue requires talking about the problem and working through it in a controlled and safe environment. Avoidance of the trauma only creates issues and will reduce a person's chance to heal and cause PTSD issues to take over their life. Another form of avoidance is to avoid people, and locations of activities that remind you of the event. An example of avoidance came up while I was in high school. A classmate was killed in a car accident and many of the students avoided visiting the corner where the person was killed.

A third symptom that doctors and psychiatrists will look for is negative changes in mood or patterns of thinking. If a person suddenly becomes constantly negative about themselves and people around them and shows a lack of ability to be positive then they may be suffering from PTSD. They may suddenly show a change in demeanor and not find joy in things they used to find joy in. They will struggle with relationships, even with family and children and become very morose. Their outlook on life will be negative and they will begin to have memory problems about the traumatic event that took place. They will be emotionally numb overall and difficult to be around. Many will avoid contact with loved ones or happy events choosing instead to be solitary and alone in their thoughts and depression.

Finally, doctors and psychiatrists will look for any extreme emotional reactions from the patient. If they suddenly start to demonstrate emotional outbursts and show very aggressive behavior or irritability then they may be suffering from PTSD. They may start to display self-destructive behavior such as speeding or drinking excessively and will have trouble concentrating on day-to-day activities. They become easily agitated and short tempered and will often have trouble sleeping. They may feel guilty about the traumatic event, especially if it included loss of life that they feel they could have prevented. Some forms of severe PTSD will cause the sufferers to consider suicide as a means to escape their issues.

The severity of all of these symptoms can vary over time, but it is important to seek professional help.

There are ways to treat PTSD and the symptoms that come along with this disorder. The first step is to get a diagnosis so that you can begin to develop a strategy to get on with your life. There is not a specific medication that will treat PTSD, but if you or your loved one are suffering from these symptoms then there are things that you can do to help them to get better. If there are secondary symptoms such as depression or anxiety, there are medications that patients can take to assist with these symptoms. The next step is to begin psychotherapy.

There are three types of therapy that are used to help treat PTSD sufferers. The first is cognitive therapy. Cognitive therapy allows a person to talk with a qualified counselor and assist them with working through the issues that they had to face during the traumatic event. Cognitive therapy is often combined with another form of therapy called exposure therapy. This type of therapy helps to cope with the traumatic event by using a virtual reality version of the event allowing you to work through the event and deal with it alongside the coaching of a qualified professional.

A third form of therapy is called eye movement desensitization and reprocessing or EMDR. This is another form of therapy that will assist people with processing an event and allow them to work through it in a more positive manner. Therapy has been proven to help people process a traumatic event and develop coping mechanisms that will allow them to return to their lives and families.

Animal Assisted Therapy for PTSD
Recently, it has become more and more popular to incorporate animals into the therapy programs for people who suffer from PTSD. Animal assisted therapy helps to overcome the extreme trauma that has caused the issue due to

the animal's unconditional love and acceptance that they provide. The animal that is paired with the patient requires care and food that requires the patient to focus on the needs of the animal and not their own needs, which can help to break the constantly recurring thoughts that many sufferers will face when they have PTSD.

Additionally, animals are accepting, non-judgmental, and will not focus on any handicap or secondary issue that the person might face as a result of their traumatic event. Animals like dogs or cats are commonly used in this type of therapy program and can often provide a warm body to curl up with when a person is facing memories of the traumatic event. Some dogs are even trained to sense the mood of their patient and to gently prod them if they start to exhibit signs of distress.

Horses have also been used in this type of therapy with considerable success. There is an advantage that PTSD sufferers get from working with a prey animal because they must learn to control their emotions and in particular fear. Horses will directly reflect the mood and feelings of their handler. If a horse senses that a person is fearful they will become fearful themselves and may run or try to escape. This response forces a person to control their feelings in order to manage their issues and provides a valuable therapy tool that the person can use to help recover from PTSD.

Typical Behaviors

People who are suffering from PTSD will display a variety of behaviors when they interact with other people. Sometimes they will seem to 'zone out' as they relive a vivid flashback of the incident and other times they may report dreams of the event. They may avoid contact with people, places or locations that make it difficult for them to not relive the event. For example, for many years after her father passed away one friend refused to visit their family home. They finally sold the home since it was so difficult for the family to adjust with all the memories of their patriarch passing from their lives so vivid in that home.

When a person has symptoms of PTSD they will often have negative changes in mood and thinking as a result. A normally happy person may suddenly become very morose and difficult to be around, while an easy going person may suddenly be very agitated and display constant mood swings and violent behavior. These changes in personality will be difficult to manage and people will need to seek professional assistance.

There is also the risk that PTSD sufferers may threaten violence against others or themselves, and these issues must be addressed quickly to avoid someone getting hurt or injured. The news is full of instances in which veterans returned to society, but were unable to re-acclimate and suffered from PTSD with no outside assistance and went on to commit a crime or commit suicide.

Example of PTSD

I remember an example many years ago when I was visiting an aunt and uncle during a thunderstorm. My entire family decided to visit since my father had just returned from Vietnam where he faced a constant barrage of bombings and air attacks. The entire time in Vietnam, he had spent listening for air raid sirens before taking cover behind barriers or in shelters. The thunderstorm began to grow louder until there was one particularly strong crash of thunder, which sent my father diving for cover underneath an end table. He laughed off the incident, but our entire family was surprised by what happened and it took him a while to get over the stress of war when he returned to our home; I remember seeing him visibly flinch during many thunderstorms during the first few years after he returned home.

The news is full of stories of veterans who returned home from overseas deployments who are having a hard time readjusting to life as a civilian. Some just enlist again to return to the environment where they are comfortable, but if that is not an option, then they are forced to return to society. But many of these people cannot let go of the trauma and issues they faced during battle. They report having issues sleeping, resorting to drugs and alcohol in order to cope, and seeing constant, vivid flashbacks of the fighting they experienced. If someone in their unit was killed they may feel an overwhelming sense of guilt for being the one who survived. Without help and support many of these PTSD sufferers end up committing suicide rather than returning to the lives that they left.

Strategies to be Effective (Family, Co-workers, Friends, Random Encounters)

Dealing with PTSD in a family member, co-worker, friend, or even in a random life encounter can sometimes be a challenge. Depending on the level of severity of the disorder, the sufferer will respond and have different symptoms and issues. Here are some tips that can be used for each one.

The first and most important thing that people must do is to seek help. If a friend or family member is suffering with PTSD they need professional assistance to learn to cope and recover successfully. A professional can help outline a treatment plan and monitor them as they go through treatment making any changes they may feel is necessary as they go through the process.

The next critical thing someone suffering with PTSD must do is to follow through on the treatment plan that has been put in place for them. Sometimes treatment may take time and patients will become frustrated when they do not see instantaneous results, but with time and consistency they will recover and move on with their lives. Encourage your friend or loved one to stay on track and follow all the instructions their doctor gives them so that they will eventually recover and get better. Be supportive of the treatment and help them to stay on track.

The next thing to do if you, a family member, or a friend suffers from PTSD is to educate yourself about the condition. Education and knowledge helps to better understand what is going on and will let you cope with the treatment plan more successfully. Understanding the recovery and treatment process will help the treatment be more effective and keep you on track for recovery.

While it can be tempting to self-medicate while you are undergoing treatment, it is important to avoid these temptations. During treatment make a point to eat a healthy diet and avoid drinking excessively. Relax and spend time with your family doing things that you enjoy. Be active in the recovery process and get out in the world as much as you can manage to help and engage with family and friends. Avoid wallowing in self-pity and seek help if you need to refocus.

Create new habits to deal with symptoms. Throughout your treatment or your loved one's treatment there will be highs and lows. When you feel down try doing something to boost your mood and to stay positive like taking a walk or trying a new hobby. By building new thought processes you will be able to break the cycle and stay positive about your treatment giving yourself the chance to get well.

Finally, if you feel alone or do not have friends or family close by then consider using a support group. Everyone can use someone to talk to and someone suffering from PTSD is no exception. Support groups will give the sufferer a network of people working through the same issue that will allow them to work through their issues and share experiences with someone else. Sharing will help the healing process and let people know that they are not alone.

Most importantly, when a family member or loved one is suffering with PTSD you must remember that they have a medical condition and it is not about you. Their condition is serious and needs help and not guilt from those who care about them. PTSD will strain any relationship and be difficult to manage, but with love and support they will be able to heal and recover.

Chapter 9: Tips for Managing a Relationship with Someone who has Avoidant Personality Disorder

Avoidant personality disorder is a condition that some people suffer that can cause them to display severe feelings of inadequacy and avoid social interactions for fear of receiving some type of negative feedback. This personality disorder often leaves people feeling unworthy and they will tend to avoid social interactions where their failures and ineptness could be exposed to the rest of the world. Studies estimate there is about 2.4 % of the general population who exhibit and suffer from this condition and its symptoms of social anxiety and lack of confidence in group situations. The issues that they face can be quite severe and will make them very anxious, lonely, and isolated from others in the world, where in truth it is only their negative self-perception that is stopping them from engaging with the rest of society. Without help, they will continue to stay isolated and miss out on the world around them and possibly having a meaningful relationship with a spouse or a family of their own.

Avoidant Personality Disorder Description

Avoidant personality disorder is most commonly found in females, but men will also exhibit the symptoms and isolation that go along with this disorder. People suffering from this condition will avoid contact with the public in any form out of fear that they could be singled out for criticism or embarrassed if they step out in public. They will often avoid forming relationships with other people and will shun contact for fear of rejection. Underlying their feelings and concerns for rejection is an overwhelming need to belong to a group, but they become overly concerned about what they see as their own shortcomings and will hide from human contact instead. They are typically overly critical of themselves and will be prone to self-loathing as they attempt to come to terms with their perceived shortcomings.

Medical Considerations and symptoms
To diagnose avoidant personality disorder, doctors and psychiatrists will look for several symptoms and behaviors. They will watch and see if a person is overly sensitive or hypersensitive to any type of criticism or rejection from others. They will look and see if the patient turns a positive remark about something into a negative criticism of themselves instead. Doctors will look to see if the patient has placed themselves in a self-imposed state of isolation where they actively avoid communication and contact with other people.

People suffering from avoidant personality disorder will often be very shy and anxious overall or anytime they are in a social situation. Many will also avoid physical contact with other human beings since, for some with this condition, physical contact has a negative connotation rather than a positive connotation. They will be mistrusting of others and not form emotional connections. They may have problems functioning in their daily lives. They display the following characteristics as well: feeling inferior to others, highly self-critical, self-loathing, social isolations, shyness, anxiety, and low self-perception.

Doctors will look at the full personality to understand if a person is suffering from this condition before making recommendations about a treatment path for the patient. Based on an overall assessment of the patient's condition and ways of interacting with society, they will come to a diagnosis of avoidant personality disorder and recommend treatment.

In some extreme cases people suffering from avoidant personality disorder may suffer from agoraphobia, or a fear of leaving the home or going into public places. This is a severe form of this disorder that requires more intensive treatment in order to overcome the symptoms and re-engage in society.

Treatment for this disorder will often involve a variety of techniques including cognitive therapy and training to develop social skills. As patients learn to work in a group environment they will add group therapy to assist them in working in a social situation and getting out of their comfort zone. It takes time to redevelop the habits that these patients have established, but with patience they can learn to rejoin society and not feel that everyone is judging their every move and action.

Typical Behaviors
People who suffer from avoidant personality disorder will be extremely sensitive to how they will be perceived by a group. This should not be confused with those who have a healthy fear of being in groups or trying something new, but instead it is a more debilitating fear of being judged or criticized. When a loved one or family member regularly shuns an engagement or leaving the home because they are shy or awkward then they may be struggling with this disease and need some help to overcome it.

People with avoidant personality disorder will typically not have a large circle of friends and will avoid social gatherings. The disorder can negatively impact their work if they are shy and scared to step out of their comfort zone and interact with new people in their business. They may be unwilling or uncomfortable getting involved with people or forming relationships and show an unhealthy preoccupation with being rejected or criticized by other people.

When people have avoidant personality disorder they will have a poor self-image and be reluctant to take risks in any situation, but in particular social situations. They will typically consider themselves very poor at communicating with other people and will let this negative self-impression stop them from engaging with people. These behaviors will last throughout a person's life until they decide to seek help for this disorder and get counseling and treatment to help them develop confidence in themselves and engage in society.

Examples of Avoidant Personality Disorder

There are people in the world that are famous that are living with avoidant personality disorder that give us examples of how a person who suffers with this condition can still be successful. For example, Kim Basinger is a successful actress who has learned to live with this condition. Ms. Basinger was diagnosed when she was young and still in school and used to describe the anxiety that she felt as so severe that her teachers thought that she was having a nervous breakdown. She eventually learned to deal with the condition and received therapy to help manage the condition.

Another star who suffered with this condition and was successful despite the issues that he faced was Donny Osmond. He once described during an interview how he would have severe stage fright and be unable to go on stage. He often described considerable performance anxiety and often said he was so scared of performing he would choose death over going on stage. This severe example of avoidant personality disorder shows just how severe the condition is and how people become incapacitated as a result of the condition.

Another famous star who struggled to overcome avoidant personality disorder was Michael Jackson. This famous singer was so particular about his performance, he would stress himself out over ensuring it was going to be perfect, losing sleep the weeks leading up to a performance. He described the issues he faced in an interview at one point and said that it was the hospitality and caring of the people around him that helped him to get through the issues he was facing.

It is often amazing how famous actors, actresses and singers are able to overcome their fears and perform in front of large audiences, but it goes to show that when people recognize the issue and seek help or get treatment they are able to overcome their disorder and be successful in life, even at the highest performance levels.

Strategies to be Effective Dealing with Avoidant Personality Disorder

Treatment and strategies for dealing with avoidant personality disorder normally include a combination of therapy and support from family and friends. Therapy will typically be in a one-on-one session versus a group setting and will require people to discuss the issues with a therapist. As treatment progresses, the patient will graduate to a group setting to help the patient learn the skills they will need to work in society. It can be a slow process, but when the patient is willing to work at improving their issues they can succeed.

Families and friends of people with avoidant personality disorder need to be understanding and supportive of the issues that their loved one is facing. They will want to include them in parties and other gatherings, but what they may not understand is that this does not help people suffering from this condition and that they must be allowed to join in with a group on their own timeline and schedule. It may seem counter-intuitive to someone who does not suffer from this condition, but this is what it will take for their friend or loved one to successfully work through their issues and join back in with family and friends. Most importantly, through all treatment people must be allowed to work at their own pace and not be pushed to exceed their comfort level.

Chapter 10: Tips for Managing a Relationship with Someone who has Borderline Personality Disorder

Borderline personality disorder has been used in a variety of ways throughout the psychiatric community and many accuse doctors and psychiatrists of using this generic label for patients who are difficult to accurately diagnose and treat. In some cases when a patient is diagnosed with borderline personality disorder it is because the doctor or psychiatrist did not know exactly where to place them in an accurate diagnosis. As a result, the borderline personality disorder came to be and became prevalent in numerous circles for being the go to diagnosis for a catch all group of symptoms.

Borderline Personality Disorder Description

Borderline personality disorders demonstrate a certain category of symptoms that have a distinct pattern. Most of these disorders center on patients who have a difficulty with interpersonal relationships and poor image of themselves. They often will be very impulsive throughout their lives and may have a mixture of symptoms that make classifying them difficult if not impossible. They will show symptoms of both psychotic behaviors and neurotic behaviors and some therapists even thought they might be cases where therapy failed to provide improvement in their condition.

Medical Considerations and symptoms

When diagnosing borderline personality disorder in patients, the doctor or psychiatrist will look at the overall patterns of instability throughout a patient's life. They will want to see a consistent pattern of instability in their relationships with other people and issues with emotion and their own self-image and how they relate within society.

People with this condition will over display a pattern of risky behaviors and may even attempt suicide at some point in their life. They will have a habit of behavior that puts them at risk like engaging in sexual acts with risky partners or attempting suicide, but not following through. Many times this personality disorder will show up in early adulthood, but it typically has gone on for years prior to them getting help. Their interpersonal history with their family and friends will show a steady history of risky behavior and there will be constant issues with their self-image and all social interactions that they engage in throughout their life.

Individuals who suffer from borderline personality disorder will be very sensitive to their environment and what is going on in their family and personal relationships. If they sense there is going to be a break up or someone is going to leave them they can become very depressed and will demonstrate profound changes in their self-image and way of thinking. They may express intense feelings of inappropriate anger and fears of abandonment that will seem unjustified to a more stable personality.

For example, patients will often panic when a therapy session is ending or be unreasonably angry if someone arrives late to an appointment with them. These issues stem from an underlying need to be with and around people at all times.

To diagnose someone with borderline personality disorder, doctors and psychiatrists will look for the following symptoms: how a person manages abandonment in their lives, this could be as simple as having a parent or loved one leave the room or judging how they would handle a hypothetical situation; how the patient perceives themselves and what type of self-image they portray to others; are there any disturbances detected. If these symptoms are detected, the patient may be suffering from borderline personality disorder.

The professionals will also want to look at how the patient manages interpersonal relationships and if they can manage a stable relationship or if they are unbalanced. They will look at how impulsive a person is and how they manage things like driving, sex, spending money, if they display routinely impulsive behavior with no controls or moderation. These too are all signs of borderline personality disorder.

People suffering from borderline personality disorder will often attempt suicide or threaten suicide and take part in frequent self-mutilation. They will describe feelings of emptiness and hollowness inside and have a difficult time controlling their anger. They may get in fights or exhibit other bad behaviors with those around them as well.

Borderline personality disorder will show up early in a person's lifetime and continue throughout their life if they do not seek treatment or get help for the condition.

Typical Behaviors
A person who is suffering from borderline personality disorder will have a series of behaviors that they will display and these behaviors are consistent throughout a person's lifetime while they are suffering with the disorder. One of the first things that people with this disorder will demonstrate can be an abnormal concern for being abandoned. They will typically go out of their way to avoid situations of abandonment and be unusually stressed if it seems they will be abandoned.

People suffering from borderline personality disorder will often be unstable in their interpersonal relationships. They will be very intense regarding their relationships and switch between extremes. Sometimes they will be characterized by extreme idealization and other times by extreme devaluation.

They will experience a severe identity disturbance and have an unstable self-image that constantly changes depending on their mood. Sufferers will typically be impulsive and take part in risky and detrimental behaviors.

Finally, they will demonstrate emotional instability with the emotions running the gambit of the emotional scales from feelings of irritability and anxiety to dysphoria and intense anger and paranoia.

Examples of Borderline Personality Disorder

There are many famous people who have suffered from borderline personality disorders and have managed to still be successful despite their diagnosis.

Doug Ferrari is the example of a famous comedian who suffered from borderline personality disorder. This comedian was many times seen with severe anger outbursts and even went so far as to beat his wife and get sent to jail. He finally decided to get some assistance for the disorder and went through extensive treatment and therapy to get his condition in line and turn his life around.

Another famous person who suffered from this disorder is the actress Angelina Jolie. She voluntarily committed herself to a neuropsychiatric institute for treatment citing an issue with suicidal tendencies. Her diagnosis was reported to be mild and she left treatment to continue on with a successful career in acting and directing as well as raising a large family with her partner Brad Pitt.

Another actress and model, Lindsay Lohan, had a history of issues from drug use and run-ins with the law to inconsistencies in her relationships with other people and her family. Her erratic behavior got her fired from many jobs and she still is struggling to turn her life around and get back on track to save her career.

Princess Diana was another famous personality who had a difficult time maintaining relationships and staying on track. She displayed a history of borderline personality disorder with cases of self-mutilation and binge eating. She frequently would cut her arms and legs when she could no longer handle the emotional issues that she constantly faced.

Each of these famous personalities struggled with their conditions and the side effects that they brought about. It directly impacted their relationships and their careers and they had a difficult time keeping their careers on track as they moved on with their lives.

Strategies to be Effective Dealing with Borderline Personality Disorder

Dealing with borderline personality disorder can be a challenge for friends and family, but one of the keys to successful rehabilitation is therapy. Long-term therapy is required to get their condition under control and to maintain their stability. Medication can also be given when they display particularly bad symptoms. These medications will help to get their symptoms under control and help to reduce the damage that they will cause to themselves as a result of their disorder.

Chapter 11: Tips for Managing a Relationship with Someone who has Schizotypal Personality Disorder

Schizotypal personality disorder is a condition where people have an extreme discomfort with interpersonal relationships and may demonstrate an extreme amount of eccentricities in their everyday relationships with other people. What happens when a person with schizotypal personality disorder tries to interact with other people is that they will misinterpret the normal interactions that other people take for granted. They will have difficulties with how they perceive the inputs they are receiving from other people and struggle with regular interactions and relationships with others.

People with schizotypal personality disorder tend to be overly superstitious. They will be convinced of the existence of paranormal activity and will believe in activities and talents that fall outside normal cultural beliefs. Ironically, people with this type of disorder will seek help for other conditions that are an offshoot of this issue and their condition may be discovered by accident.

Schizotypal Personality Disorder Description

A recent study once showed that schizotypal personality disorder symptoms were present in about 3.9 percent of a population. Schizotypal personality disorder is a condition that causes people to deviate from the normal accepted patterns and beliefs of society or an individual's culture. Their skewed view on society will make them perceive everyday situations quite differently than the remainder of society and their distorted views will impact how they function around others. They may have issues with impulse control in social situations and their condition will impact their work and social functioning in multiple areas. Onset of these issues can be traced back to when the person was younger and they will demonstrate a long history throughout their life of having suffered from these symptoms.

Medical Considerations and symptoms

The symptoms that doctors and psychiatrists will look for when diagnosing this condition include issues with forming close relationships with the people around them. People with schizotypal personality disorder will have issues forming close relationships both with family and friends because their altered view on society will make it difficult for others to understand them. Their perception of the world is often so skewed that it will make others uncomfortable around them and force them to suspect their sanity and mental health.

People with schizotypal personality disorder will tend to have a twisted reference system that may include delusional thoughts in these references that will leave people without the same viewpoint in the dark. Those who try to get close to these people will often be puzzled trying to understand their point of reference and may finally give up in frustration and abandon their efforts in trying to establish a meaningful relationship. The person with the condition will also be puzzled by other's responses because to them their version of reality is the norm and they will struggle to understand why others do not see the world as they do.

When a person suffers from schizotypal personality disorder they will have unusual perceptions of everyday experiences even down to the reactions of their own body with their daily life. They will believe in telekinesis, clairvoyance, and telepathy as well as believe that a sixth sense exists within the world. Children and adolescents with this condition will often have random, bizarre fantasies and be overly concerned and preoccupied with the supernatural world.

As the disease progresses and people go through life with this condition they may develop an extreme anxiety with social situations because of a long history of unacceptance within society. They become paranoid and suspicious of everyone around them and will not form meaningful long-term relationships outside of immediate family, who will also struggle to understand them.

This disorder is often not diagnosed until a person is in adulthood because some of these traits can be seen in all young adults as they go through life and develop a personality of their own. It is only after their anxiety around social situations and secondary conditions start to show up that many people will seek help for this disorder and finally receive a diagnosis.

Researchers and doctors have not been able to identify a direct cause for schizotypal personality disorder, but they do have theories about how and when it shows up within someone's personality. They believe that there is a biological or genetic factor involved as well as an environmental one that can trigger the condition. Researchers do agree however, that there is most likely a series of conditions that combine to trigger the symptoms. There are also some studies that show that the condition can be passed down to children. Parents who have the condition will tend to have children that have the condition, however, some doctors and psychiatrists think that with the children of parents with schizotypal personality disorder they have learned the skewed behavior as a norm rather than a condition, hence they see it as normal rather than atypical behavior.

Treatment for schizotypal personality disorder will typically revolve around a combination of medication for the secondary symptoms that develop and therapy for the primary causes. Through conversation and discussion trained therapists are able to help people with this disorder to come to grips with the issues they face dealing with reality as a whole and they will help them learn social skills so that they may better integrate into society. Many times therapy will involve learning coping skills rather than trying to change their perceptions and teaching the patient what is acceptable within society as a whole. Therapy does not try and change their position or views, but instead teaches them how to cope and manage relationships within society so that they can be effective, hold a job, and be productive members of society.

Typical Behaviors
The behaviors of someone who has schizotypal personality disorder will not be particularly damaging or life threatening to the individual or society as a whole, but will be seen by others as unusual, strange, and often very peculiar.

People with this disorder will seem to have a distorted sense of reality and accept the abnormal as an everyday occurrence. For example, as mentioned previously they will be convinced that they can communicate telepathically with others. Their beliefs will be very firm that they have this talent and there will be very little others can do to disprove their ideas. Others with these symptoms will believe they have other supernatural talents and accept their view on the world as the norm. People with this condition will often be seen as odd or very peculiar, but many exist within our schools, work, and even home life. They have often learned that their ideas are not understood or accepted by mainstream society and as a result will not share their thoughts and ideas with others for fear of rejection or social issues.

People with this condition often learn to cope with their ideals and often feel excluded from the world around them as a result. When they meet new people it is difficult for them to establish long friendships as once they truly open up about their eccentric views on the world, most people will not understand and will abandon them. Some are lucky enough to accept their off-center view on the world and they are capable of forming relationships where people accept them for who they are and how they interact with the world.

Those who do not find an understanding group of friends can develop secondary conditions that will severely impact their lives and mental stability. They will become very closed in and not be able to open up to others. They will become anxious and paranoid about how others will perceive them in the world and will be afraid to leave their own homes where they feel sheltered and protected.

Even their manner of speech can be skewed which is a dead giveaway to others that they may be a little off kilter and will drive others away. It is unfortunate that people in society have built in radar that will detect someone who does not fit the "accepted norms." As a result, people stay away from this type of personality. But if people open up and see that they just have a skewed version and see things differently, then they are capable of having strong and loyal relationships.

Examples of Schizotypal Personality Disorder

People with schizotypal personality disorder do exist within society and are able to effectively live and work within societal norms. One example of a famous person who succeeded with this condition is Emily Dickinson. Ms. Dickinson was a famous poet who lived in Massachusetts during the 1800s. Despite her psychological condition, she was gifted at writing and wrote numerous poems throughout her lifetime, though all as she was secluded in her home. She did receive treatment for her condition and was able to fully recover and her poems inspired other people with the condition to seek help.

Vincent Van Gogh, the famous painter, was also suspected of having schizotypal personality disorder. His paintings and expressions within his art helped him to work through some of the issues with his condition, although throughout his life he preferred to be alone rather than have to deal with other people.

Another person who is rumored to have schizotypal personality disorder (though it will not be diagnosed or revealed because it would threaten his position as a leader within the country) is Kim Jong II. This tyrannical leader of the North Korean country demonstrated a total lack of interest in socializing with other people. He is completely closed off as a leader and does not want anyone around him who will threaten his position or challenge him. He views his leadership as a great accomplishment rather than the dictatorship that it truly is and the people in his country are almost forced to sing their praises of the country or face severe retribution. His son, who has assumed his rule after his death, is rumored to have a similar condition.

Strategies to be Effective Dealing with Schizotypal Personality Disorder

Families, friends, and co-workers of people with schizotypal personality disorder will have often developed an understanding of the condition that their loved one is facing. Many will have learned coping mechanisms that will accept their loved one's eccentric view on life and allow them to engage with them on another level. They will typically accept the eccentricities and can listen patiently as they discuss something that they may not understand, but is important to their loved one.

Families are key to successfully managing this condition for two reasons. First, there is evidence that the skewed view of reality can be learned from childhood. This means that adults who have schizotypal personality disorder can have children with this condition and will raise them up with the same twisted view on reality. Because of this possibility, it is estimated that the total percentage of people that suffer from this personality disorder that go untreated is much higher than the estimated 3.6 percent of the population. It is only when someone is rejected from a group that they may develop secondary conditions and seek medical help, but if their whole world accepts them for who they are they will never need to seek assistance.

Tolerance and understanding without judgment are key to successfully managing a relationship with someone who has schizotypal personality disorder and with this compassion they will soon see that these people have a considerable amount of love to share and can be genuine and open people in a relationship. People just need to be accepted for who they are and not judged so that they can form long lasting relationships and engage in society.

Chapter 12: Tips for Managing a Relationship with Someone who is Passive Aggressive

Have you ever looked at someone who made you so frustrated you just shook your head? That person who caused you so much frustration every time you had to deal with them that you figured it must have been something that you did wrong. Or have you just given up trying to understand someone's behavior because it was just bizarre? If any of these situations sound even vaguely familiar, then you just might have had an encounter with someone who is passive aggressive.

Even something as simple as giving a compliment can have a different meaning with someone who is passive aggressive. They may say that someone looks great and did they do something different with their hair. When the person asks for clarification they will say something sarcastic like, "it is amazing you get it to stay that way" and if you ask for more clarification or even confront them about the odd comment they will only look at you funny as if you did not understand. This is the mode of operation for someone that exhibits passive aggressive behavior; they will say things that could be interpreted as mean, but say them in a more sarcastic and condescending way to give them a double meaning open to interpretation.

The problem is, how do you know when they are being genuine and when they are actually insulting you?

Passive aggressive behavior is not a mental condition or disorder, but is a learned behavior from people who have a difficulty expressing negative opinions and feelings towards others. When someone has this behavior pattern they will outwardly agree with an instruction, but instead of following through, they will choose not to follow instructions rather than confronting the person as a way of expressing their disproval. This behavior type can make it very difficult for people to have meaningful relationships and will impact their jobs and life as a whole since, rather than dealing with the issue, they use their passive aggressive behavior as a way of avoiding conflict and dealing with other people.

Description of Passive Aggressive Behavior

A person who has passive aggressive behavior patterns will typically be someone who has issues dealing with negative feelings and emotions. They will often say and appear to mean one thing but their true feelings and actions are completely the opposite. It can be very difficult for someone to understand a person's behavior when they act in this manner since society, as a whole, generally accepts a person for what they say they will do.

Take for example, a situation between a husband and a wife. The husband asks the wife if she will do something for him and she agrees, but then never follows through or constantly procrastinates until he does the job himself. These behaviors are often the result of resentment or anger towards the other party or even a hostile attitude. These behaviors can develop over time when there is a poor or unfair relationship, one or the other party feels that they are not appreciated or that they have been cheated on. They may resent the other person for constantly making demands on their time or feel there is an unbalanced work load or responsibilities within the relationship. There could be a multitude of causes for their feelings, but the result is that the person uses a passive aggressive nature to display their displeasure rather than directly addressing the situation with their partner.

There can be many reasons they choose this path such as conversations in the past were ineffective; they feel threatened or trapped in the relationship, or powerless to make any changes for the better. It can be a difficult place for a person to be in, especially if they use this behavior as a survival mechanism instead of seeking help.

Spotting a passive aggressive person can be easy by looking for four key characteristics in their behaviors with others. First, they will seem very unreasonable to deal with and people will have a hard time understanding where they are coming from. The second characteristic that passive aggressive people have is that they make people uncomfortable to be around and others will leave them thinking that was an extremely unpleasant experience. A third trait that this personality type will have is that they will rarely express their hostility directly towards another person, but will seem hostile when someone approaches them like they have a 'chip on their shoulder'. Finally, for a person to be characterized as passive aggressive they repeat the same behavior patterns over and over. Everyone at some point in their life may resort to passive aggressive behavior, but when it becomes an ongoing pattern within their lives, then it becomes a problem and should be addressed before it negatively impacts their relationships, job, and life as a whole.

Typical Behaviors of Passive Aggressiveness

Passive aggressive behavior is not actually classified as a medical condition, but there is a behavior type that psychiatrists and doctors use to typify their actions and better understand the person as a whole.

Passive aggressive speech and behaviors is a subtle way to try and control someone who they feel is out of their control. It is a power struggle where one party feels powerless but tries to gain the upper hand through passive aggressive comments and expressing anger in a very indirect, often misinterpreted manner. Using this subtle and less direct form of communication the passive aggressive personality is able to attack their target without putting themselves at risk of retribution while giving themselves an out if their target realizes what is happening and challenges them about what they said.

For example, consider the following situation: a couple goes to a restaurant for a nice dinner. The woman orders a salad and a glass of red wine while the man orders a steak cooked medium rare, baked potato with all the toppings, and an appetizer of greasy potato skins with several pints of beer. The woman then looks at the food that the man ate and makes a comment like, "you are so lucky you can eat all that food without gaining weight or impacting your health, I'm not that fortunate!" What she really meant by saying that was "you are going to get fat and have a heart attack eating like that." The woman tries to hide her resentment in what appears to be a compliment about how fortunate the man is to be able to eat without concern but left the comment open to interpretation as to whether she was really sincere. If the man challenged her statement she would most likely look at him with hurt eyes and say that he took it wrong. In a healthy relationship, the woman would express her concern for his health and give advice on a better choice for his meal. Of course, this would be a no win situation for the woman as the man would most likely just outright ignore her comments which makes the entire incident frustrating for both parties. This is an example of passive aggressive behavior and the reasons why one party may choose to use this method of communication when dealing with another.

Dealing with a passive aggressive exchange can be challenging in every relationship because there is always the cheap way out for people to say that they were misunderstood. Instead of being honest and open about what they are feeling, they will instead continue the charade and let it escalate.

Consider another example of a man and wife who are trying to pick a restaurant for a night on the town. The man begins by asking where the woman would like to go and she responds that she does not care and for him to choose. The man will say OK and drive them to the bar on the corner for wings and beer. When they arrive at the bar, the woman will appear upset and start to pout so the man will ask her what's wrong and she'll answer she does not like that bar and wanted a nice Italian restaurant. The man will get frustrated as she continues by saying he should have known she didn't like that bar and essentially should have read her mind on what she felt like eating that night. The man will then offer to go to the Italian restaurant to which the woman replies, no it is too late, and I will find something I can eat here. Needless to say, they are in for an unpleasant evening at that bar.

It is ironic that many passive aggressive communications are between opposite sexes where the woman is afraid to confront her partner for some perceived lack of power. But the irony is, the woman has considerable power because the last thing the man wants is for her to be unhappy! It is unfortunate that many women cannot understand this simple fact and instead choose to play mind games with their partner using a passive aggressive strategy to attempt to gain control of the other person through manipulation.

There are different types of passive aggressive behaviors that people exhibit and each one has a different motivation. Some passive aggressive behaviors are motivated by malicious intent. They may have bad feelings due to a bad day at work or they got stuck in traffic and then want to take those passive aggressive feelings out on someone. Often family, friends, or a spouse are the recipients of this behavior and may take the full brunt of the frustrations someone feels as a result of their bad day. This type of behavior will just cause resentment by the recipient and they may intentionally misinterpret the situation to make it seem like an attack. For example, a woman comes home from work to find her husband playing video games with the kids. She walks in with a huff and asks why the trash is still piled up in the hallway waiting to be taken out. The man, resenting her tone of voice, yells back at her to quit nagging at him, he will get it when he is done with his game. The woman grabs the trash with a huff and walks out mumbling how she is the only one who does anything around the house. While there is some justification and anger behind the exchange, the manner in which it was handled was passive aggressive and resulted in unnecessary anger and frustration on both parts.

Another type of passive aggressive behavior motivations are those that are unintentionally hurtful. This type of communication is where one party does not want to be hurtful, but forms their message in a subterfuge way that makes their meaning quite clear that they mean the exact opposite of what they are saying.

For example, consider another relationship example between a man and a woman. They have been in the relationship for quite some time and the woman feels it is about time they talk about marriage. She begins dropping hints about marriage or making indirect suggestions about the topic in a frustrated manner. Instead of understanding the hints, the man just gets the message that she is frustrated and instead thinks that she is tired of the relationship and asks if she wants to see other people. As a result, feelings are hurt unintentionally because both parties did not clearly articulate what they wanted from the other.

Most passive aggressive behavior can be avoided through open and honest conversation, but whatever the reason, people are reluctant to communicate directly and instead try to drop hints in their conversations, which make miscommunication an issue.

Examples of Passive Aggressive Personalities

Passive aggressive personality types can be found in both our everyday world and throughout history. They inundate our lives with their behaviors while trying to get us to do something for them.

Consider a flyer that was sent out by a direct mail campaign to help fight world hunger. On the outside of the envelope was a picture of a starving child with the words "throw me away, I'm used to it." Or consider the hint that some parents who were funding a wedding for their daughter sent with these comments in a note to "protect our investment, buy a scale."

Even children have learned how to be passive aggressive with this young student's note to his mother about his lunch saying "I love you mom, but tomorrow I want to buy a school lunch." Or the suitor who proposed on an empty toilet paper roll adding the comment "you will never see this because you never change the roll".

Passive aggressive actions are engrained in our society and you can find examples at all levels of human behavior. Protests are even a sign of passive aggressive behavior.

Consider the great leader Mahatma Ghandi who went on an extensive hunger strike and protest against Great Britain to help lead India to independence. These protests were a form of passive aggressive behavior that led to the freedom of India and inspired other forms of nonviolent protest across the world. Unfortunately, part of Ghandi's message was lost on some more inappropriate protestors who would protest for inappropriate reasons at the funerals of slain people.

No matter how people use passive aggressive behavior there is a healthier way to communicate and get your message across to the intended recipient and using effective communication is the first place to start.

Treatment Strategies for Passive Aggressive Behaviors

So how do you effectively manage someone who is habitually passive aggressive? How do you drop all the pretenses and actually communicate rather than being frustrated and fighting?

In order to get over the passive aggressive tendencies that happen in some interactions with other people, consider some of these ideas. First, why does the person use a passive aggressive communication style? Does this style of communication have a better chance of success and getting them what they want from the interaction? If someone has developed the habit of always communicating in this manner, and worse yet, seems to always get what they want as a result, then it is time to stop this behavior immediately.

In order to improve this interaction you must ask the person to change their behavior and the best way to do this is to ask them to reword the question so that you understand what it is they are asking. This will be difficult at first, but if you look below the surface you will find the true meaning while you ignore the inferences of how they say something.

This will be difficult! But remember, you are trying to help this person and make your interactions with them more effective and less passive aggressive.

The next step in dealing with passive aggressive behavior is to refuse to reward them for their attack. This could be getting you angry or making you do something for them, but until they ask you directly do not be tempted to give in to their subtlety until they remove the passive aggressive undertones of what they are saying. People will soon realize when their behavior is backfiring and will modify what they are saying to not appear childish and stupid.

Another step to remember when dealing with a passive aggressive personality is that you must never directly confront the person. If you attack them they will become very defensive and it is unlikely they will admit that they were wrong about the situation. Consider this conversation again between a man and a wife: the wife looks at what the man is wearing and says, "you shouldn't wear that because you are getting too fat." The man looks at her and says "you hurt my feelings when you call me fat." The wife then defends herself by saying "I only tell you that because I am worried about your health," to which the man replies "but it hurts my feeling when you call me names," and the wife replies again "you are too sensitive." The man again then emphasizes his feelings. This conversation could continue for hours where the wife did not intend to hurt his feelings, but her harsh passive aggressive comments were unnecessary if she would have used a different approach to relay her message.

While it can be easy to fall into the trap of passive aggressive behavior, in order to have truly adult communication you must work through this pattern and address the underlying cause for the communication issue that is not being addressed.

It will be difficult to change a long-established pattern of behaviors with your family, significant other, or loved one, but it can be done with just a little practice and focus. In this case it is helpful to get the other person on board with these changes to avoid getting into a passive aggressive exchange about being passive aggressive.

Chapter13: Other Random Issues and Disorders

Psychological behaviors and unusual people can be found everywhere throughout our lives. From the dinner table to the workplace, these unusual behaviors exist all around us. Having said that, here are some more mentally ill issues people you may come across in your day-to-day life may be confronted with.

Eating Disorders

Eating out is a fun diversion from everyday life and let's you try new foods from new chefs with different ideas on how to prepare a culinary masterpiece. But when you have someone with an eating disorder, dining out can become an exercise in futility as you try to break down the menu item into all its components to ensure all the ingredients are acceptable to whomever accompanied you to the restaurant.

If you have ever worked in the food service industry, you can understand how difficult it is when someone has to make a change to the menu. Most upscale restaurants can easily accommodate changes to the menu such as ordering salad dressing on the side, but many fast food chains cannot manage these changes since food arrives prepackaged and prepared. So, if you find that you or a family member has a variety of food related issues that require you to scrutinize the menu then consider trying new recipes at home to ensure that all dietary restrictions are met.

Eating disorders come in all shapes, varieties, and conditions and range from those who just choose not to eat certain foods to those who have a legitimate psychological condition regarding the foods they eat. Managing eating disorders with the people you come in contact with in your life requires sensitivity and understanding to avoid embarrassing the person or sometimes even triggering a medical condition.

Picky Eaters

Everyone has a story about a picky eater, from the college roommate who refused to eat anything except bacon and boiled spaghetti to the friend who dated a woman who would turn up her nose at a beautiful steak dinner and instead would only eat Chicken McNuggets and French fries. Fortunately, human beings are omnivores and evolution has made it so we can survive on a variety of different foods, but obviously, these limited diet options would not be nutritionally balanced.

Picky eating actually begins when we are younger and if we are not introduced to a variety of foods at that time we begin to stick to those foods we know that are safe and avoiding food we are not familiar with. Human beings have an inherent trait where anything that is unknown may be dangerous so we avoid it in order to survive.

The degree to which some people avoid foods varies greatly. Some will eat almost anything that they can put in their mouths, while others will only try small bites of food and then judge how they feel afterwards to determine if they will try those foods again. There are even cultures that are dedicated to eating foods that many find repulsive and they will have celebrations where these foods are the primary ones served.

Consider the Asian fruit durian; this smelly food is so pungent that it is against the law to carry it in many public places. I had the opportunity to try this fruit while in China, but was so repulsed by the smell that I could barely take a bite and then the taste was not much better and I could not wait to rid my mouth of that unpleasant flavor. However, my friends in Asia loved the fruit and declared it one of the richest and delicious foods ever tasted. I had to wash my hands of that experience and assume that they had been brought up developing an appreciation for that fruit.

Almost everyone has encountered a picky eater at some point in their life from the small child who cannot be tempted to try a new type of food to the co-worker who turns up their nose at a non-traditional dish at a potluck. While it is polite to at least try a bite of something new, it usually is best to just avoid the behavior and revel in the fact that if someone is not interested in trying a new food that you have prepared then there will be more left over for you to eat.

While picky eaters do have a psychological background there are typically no medical repercussions that other eating disorders will have. Picky eaters will be a normal weight and will appear healthy eating their chosen diet. If you meet someone new it is always suggested that you ask about any eating habits before spending money on an expensive dish they will probably not eat. Look on the bright side, also, Chicken McNuggets are much less expensive than a good quality Filet Mignon so your date will save you money in the long run with their choice of food!

Food Aversions
Who doesn't enjoy a good meal or sitting down and sharing a holiday meal with family and friends? Surprisingly, a large portion of the world population with eating disorders! While most of the world enjoys eating and sharing a meal with loved ones, there is a portion of our population that shuns food in all its forms and goes to great lengths to avoid consuming any type of nourishment or avoids a particular type of food.

I remember when I was growing up and every year during Lent, a Catholic tradition, we would be forced to give up something for Lent to assimilate the sacrifice that Jesus gave when he gave his life for us. For forty days we were forced to go without this item or activity in the hopes that it would make us more pious and spiritual. However, this activity actually had the opposite effect for some in my family. One aunt in particular, decided to give up eating meat for Lent and consumed only vegetables and an occasional piece of chicken; however, what ended up happening when she avoided this type of food was that she developed an aversion to it and instead of the pious act of giving up something we enjoyed for the celebration of Lent, she developed a food aversion that radically changed her diet so that she no longer enjoyed sharing food with the remainder of the family.

Food aversions can be developed through diet and habit and should not be confused with food allergies which are a serious medical condition. Food allergies or other sensitivities can be difficult to manage, but are completely different than those with a psychological issue which does not allow people to eat certain types of food. There are instances where food aversions can display medical symptoms after a person has gone for an extended period of time without that food; sometimes these aversions can almost resemble food allergies so people must be careful.

Managing food aversions and allergies usually just requires awareness and understanding. Any chef wants people to appreciate the food that he/she prepares so rather than preparing something they may not want to eat, simply ask if there are any food allergies or preferences before you prepare a meal or choose a restaurant. People with food allergies will often pre-emptively warn you of their allergies, but you may have to dig a little further to discover food aversions since this type of eating disorder is typically hidden by the person by simply not choosing that type of food to put on their plate.

Anorexia, Bulimia and Binge Eating
There are a group of eating disorders that are serious psychological conditions including anorexia nervosa, bulimia nervosa, and binge eating disorder. Each of these disorders can cause serious physical problems and are often accompanied by a constant concern with weight and appearance.

Anorexia
People with anorexia will often refuse to eat and say they are not hungry. They suffer from a negative self-image and will constantly be exercising and trying to improve their appearance. People suffering from anorexia will

avoid situations where they would be forced to eat in order to fit in and will also appear unusually thin and gaunt in appearance with many negative side-effects from the lack of food. Treating this condition requires medical help and intervention in order for people to relearn good habits.

If you encounter someone who is recovering from anorexia you will want to be supportive and help to boost his or her self-esteem. Encourage them to take part in activities that will be rewarding and avoid glorifying food and eating. Take a casual approach to meals and treat them as matter-of-fact events. Avoid situations where they might trigger the behaviors that brought on the condition, but instead keep the lifestyle and activities healthy in nature. Most importantly, avoid being judgmental; no amount of praise will correct their self-image or fix the issue, instead you must redirect and assist them to develop a more positive outlook on life.

Bulimia
Bulimia nervosa is similar to anorexia in that it is a legitimate psychological condition that has a direct impact on the health and well-being of the person. The symptoms and signs to watch for with bulimia are when a person will binge eat to the point where they are in pain, self-induced vomiting or purging after eating, they will tend to exercise quite excessively, and begin to

develop symptoms of malnutrition such as bleeding gums, irregular heart beat, and swollen glands to name just a few of the extensive physical symptoms. People suffering from bulimia will appear to have a healthy body weight and some are actually overweight, but will typically have a very negative body image. During meals you will often see they get up multiple times to go to the bathroom where they may even purge their food just to return and continue eating.

In order to treat these conditions people will need psychotherapy to help them to relearn healthy, normal eating habits. This type of therapy is called cognitive therapy which focuses on relearning healthy behaviors and will often involve family and loved ones to provide the support that they need. The support of family and friends is key to helping people overcome these eating disorders because many times a feeling of inadequacy helped drive them to low self-esteem which is a stepping stone to eating disorder issues.

Binge-Eating
Binge-eating is another type of eating disorder that can show up with all types of people. Do not confuse this with the type of eating that occurs around the holidays which is seasonal. People suffering from this condition will regularly eat to the point of pain and take no steps to eliminate

the additional calories through exercise or by purging. People who suffer from this condition will often turn to food for comfort and will sit for long periods, alone, eating any food that they can find. They will typically feel very depressed and disgusted by their behavior, but be powerless to stop it.

Helping a friend or loved one who constantly binges requires that you help them rebuild their self-esteem and find a more useful outlet when they are feeling down or depressed. Food has become a virtual pacifier and something they turn to when they have emotions they cannot deal with through other means so they need help in redirecting these feelings into a better outlet. It helps to introduce them to new activities where they can be successful and find happiness in a positive behavior rather than comfort in a negative behavior.

Mild Autism

Another condition that is showing up more frequently in day-to-day life is autism or autism spectrum disorder (ASD). Because of the wide range of diagnosis within the umbrella of this disorder, the medical community now describes the symptoms as a spectrum ranging from very mild cases where people can successfully interact with society to the full out disorders where people have difficulty performing even the most basic functions needed in order to survive. The diagnosis for autism normally shows up during childhood and is seen as developmental issues when the child is young or they have difficulty showing emotions and forming emotional bonds, even with close family members.

When I was growing up we had the opportunity to work with a variety of foster children from a local group home. Many of these children were in the foster care system due to issues with their families and home life not being able to care for them. While some of the issues were with the parents having poor parenting skills, some of the others were due to the children themselves, including one child who suffered from mild autism. This child was a challenge to deal with in our home because his behaviors were completely different than what was expected from normal children and, as can be expected, this resulted in him being teased at school.

However, like most children he still wanted to fit in with his peers and would take any suggestion that his classmates gave him with no filters for socially acceptable behavior. One day during lunch in the school cafeteria he was given the suggestion to do his best Michael Jackson dancing impression in the middle of the lunchroom. He did his best, which resembled a robot having spasms, which ended up with more teasing from the children that he tried to impress.

Adults with autism have normally developed coping mechanisms to allow them to interact with society and be functioning adults. We will often encounter people with autism in our daily lives and not even realize that they have this condition, but there are signs that do show up. For example, you may see a family member or friend who shies away from any type of physical contact, fails to make eye contact, or speaks in an unusual pattern.

People with autism may seem to have no emotions which can be very disconcerting for some people when something happens that would normally elicit an emotional response and they will be completely oblivious to the emotions of those around them. For example, when a co-worker announced that she was sad due to the loss of her beloved dog, her news was met with sympathy and compassion from those around her while a co-worker with mild autism just wanted to know when the report she was working on would be complete. The responses of someone with mild autism may seem cold and uncaring or even robotic, but we must remember that they process emotions differently and we must accept their responses and not take offense.

Autism spectrum disorder can be difficult to understand, but with patience we can accept that everyone does think and process things differently, those with autism are just more visible. Just remember that those with autism do not have the same social filters that others have and their response may not be as you expect them to be.

Depression

People who suffer from depression may be some of the most difficult to identify since one of the symptoms includes withdrawing from society and losing interest in the world around them. Identifying the symptoms of depression often requires someone close to the person such as a family member or friend recognizing the symptoms and helping them.

Depression is a medical condition that affects a person's mood and causes them to constantly feel sad and to no longer be interested in life or even things that used to bring them enjoyment. They will typically stop doing the things that they enjoyed like hobbies or outdoor activities and instead will struggle with managing even day-to-day life and activities. People suffering from depression may have any of the following symptoms that will help to identify the issue that they are suffering: angry outbursts, easily frustrated, insomnia, lack of energy, changes in appetite, anxiety, memory issues, and sometimes even discuss suicide. Depression is a medical condition that requires help and you should encourage anyone who demonstrates these symptoms to seek medical attention.

But how do we manage this issue in our everyday lives? Depression is not something that is often seen and may not be recognized from casual interactions. People with depression will turn inwards and not seek help from others, especially casual interactions. They will avoid places where they will be expected to be cheerful and will often cancel out of parties or special events, instead choosing solitude and staying home. If a friend or family member seems to be regularly missing from activities then they may be suffering from depression. This condition can sneak up into our relationships and go unnoticed for a considerable amount of time.

Clinical depression should not be confused with a normal emotion of feeling down. If someone has experienced a loss or gone through a bad experience it is normal for them to be sad and to take some time to deal with their emotions in a healthy manner. It's when they are not able to process these emotions that it can turn into depression.

Attention Deficit and Hyperactivity Disorder (ADHD)

Attention Deficit and Hyperactivity Disorder or ADHD is a condition that is being diagnosed quite frequently today in children, but can also show up in adults as well. ADHD is displayed when someone routinely has difficulty focusing on one thing, either a task or topic and demonstrates very impulsive behavior that impacts their performance at work, school and in relationships. When symptoms show up in children they often continue into adulthood making these people sometimes lag behind others in succeeding in life. Some people with ADHD will not even be aware that they have it, which means they must interact in daily life without treatment or coping mechanisms, leaving other people to essentially deal and manage their symptoms.

You can recognize people with ADHD when you find someone that has a difficult time focusing on a task, they will be fidgety and have a hard time sitting still, they will start something and not follow it through to completion often leaving many small tasks in various stages of completion and they will struggle in their relationships with other people due to issues with mood swings and low tolerances for being frustrated.

If a family member or other loved one is demonstrating signs of ADHD there are things you can do to better interact with them and to support them with their issues. First, let them know your observations in a calm and loving way. They may not be aware of what they are doing if their behaviors have continued for a very long time. Offer to help them seek medical help or go to counseling to teach them ways to better manage their symptoms and do well in their everyday lives. Some accommodations must be made to help deal with this disorder and with just a little help you can help people with ADHD to overcome these issues and be successful.

ADHD is highly treatable and there are many famous people who have succeeded even when having to deal with this disorder. The famous Olympic swimmer Michael Phelps focused his ADHD treatment using swimming as a medium and became a multiple gold medal winner in that event. The comedian and actress Whoopi Goldberg was also diagnosed and was able to overcome those issues and be quite successful.

There are multiple examples of people with ADHD in the world that were able to successfully manage their condition and go on and achieve success, but how do we deal with these people in our everyday lives?

One of the most disturbing issues that you will encounter when dealing with people with ADHD is misinterpreting their behaviors as being disinterested. You will find that they appear to be listening to what you have to say, but if you ask them to repeat back any of the words they may have only caught the very last sentence. If you have a family member or child who is diagnosed with ADHD one of the first things you will want to remember is that they will need constant reminders to ensure that they heard an important message.

Consider using effective communication strategies by first telling them what you are going to tell them, repeat what you just told them then summarize the key points. At first this may seem redundant but you will find that your communication improves and there is less frustration in your everyday life. You can also encourage your loved one to repeat back what was just said to ensure they understood the message. This is another communication strategy that will help to manage relationships with someone who has ADHD.

ADHD can be difficult to live with, but there are techniques and treatment available. Consider using these techniques with someone who is diagnosed with ADHD to help preserve your own sanity or when there is important business to be done.

Obsessive Compulsive Disorder (OCD)

Obsessive Compulsive Disorder or OCD is a personality disorder that can range from a low level annoying habit to an irrational thought or fear that debilitates a person. OCD exists to some extent in every person and is actually a survival mechanism that has evolved in humans over time. Consider a nighttime routine where you tuck your children into bed checking that windows are closed and locked and all doors to the home are locked and secured or maybe even arming a home alarm system. Many people go through this nightly routine to protect themselves and their family and will not sleep until they check and recheck each door and window. This type of OCD can be easily managed and is seen quite frequently.

The type of OCD that becomes debilitating is when a person spends all night walking back and forth to ensure the door has been locked or picks up another disturbing habit such as washing and rewashing their hands multiple times to ensure they are clean. Since most people with OCD will not recognize a habit as an issue, many will not seek treatment to help with their condition.

The symptoms you must watch for when you suspect a person may have OCD is to look for both compulsions and obsessions in their behaviors. These behaviors may cause the person to become nervous or very agitated if they are not able to follow through on them, which can develop additional disorders when they try to refrain from the activity. People with OCD typically do not like to see things dirty and will want everything to be symmetrical and orderly. For example, a misplaced tile in a flooring pattern can drive a person with OCD furious because they want everything to be in order. When people suffer from OCD, they can have secondary obsessions related to their primary compulsions such as a fear of touching people for risk of getting germs or thinking that an appliance was left on even when someone visibly checks if the appliance is turned off. OCD sufferers will avoid situations where they cannot attend to their obsessions and will often lead a sheltered life as they can become afraid to leave their home.

Managing a relationship with someone who has OCD will depend on the level to which they suffer the symptoms. It is fine to laugh at a partner or significant other who has to check the home alarm system and lock the doors twice each night because deep down, you know that you are safe, but when your loved one gets up throughout the night to check the door then it is time to get help.

Summary and Closing Tips

We have now had a chance to review a multitude of personality and psychological disorders and the specific symptoms and treatments that are available to better manage these conditions to live with each of these people.

From the antisocial and off beat nature of the psychopath to the actions that can potentially cross the line that a sociopath exhibits, we now have the tools to better manage our actions with each of these irrational types of people.

If you come across a self-involved narcissist, you will know better than to criticize them and to shatter their fragile ego that clings to a thin thread. Instead, you can allow them their vanity and redirect their focus to the task at hand.

If you encounter someone with the highs and lows of bipolar disorder, you can now better understand what this type of person is going through as they struggle in their daily lives to get better. You will have the tools you need to interact with them and know how to watch for signs that could trigger their emotional highs and lows.

When you encounter someone with multiple personality disorder you can better relate to their complete separation from the world and understand the issues they face watching the world while being trapped inside their own bubble. Or if you wonder why someone is acting strangely, they just might be experiencing another persona invading their own.

Neuroses are helpful and can protect us from danger, but when they consume our lives then it is time to get treatment. Even the most insignificant act could trigger a neurotic episode that impacts your daily life in varying degrees.

If you have a family member that is obsessed with being sick or seeing the doctor for more tests, then you just might be dealing with a hypochondriac. This condition can consume a person's life and test the sanity of friends and family members, but just remember to remove the medical section from the newspaper each time it arrives to limit their ammunition for future issues and conditions.

When people experience a highly traumatic event it can leave their psyche damaged when they return to their normal lives. Sometimes the condition is so severe they could be suicidal and require many years of therapy and supportive care. Remember to be there and support your friends and family if they suffer from PTSD; they will appreciate your support and lack of judgment while they work to get their symptoms under control and get on with their life.

If a friend or family member shows symptoms of avoidant personality disorder, you will now understand why their shyness is difficult for them to overcome by themselves or you can now better see how those with borderline personality disorder are struggling to control their risk tendencies to start harming themselves.

People with schizotypal personality disorder will be happy to know that the world is now more aware of their condition and hopefully people will be more understanding of the issues they face as they try to engage with the world as a whole. Instead of judging them for their unusual quirks and weird perceptions of reality, they will happily embrace them and welcome their different views on the world.

Dealing with a passive aggressive personality can be one of the most difficult situations you will face in any type of relationship. People seem to relish the opportunity to be indirect and instead leave their words open to interpretation or better yet, misinterpretation! With a few steps that we described in this book, you can reclaim your conversations with your significant other, family member, or even a coworker and essentially cut through the misinterpretations and find what they are really trying to say to you.

Make sure not to get drawn into their trap of passive aggressive communication with a malicious intent and let them hide behind the excuse that you do not understand. Cut to the chase and get to the heart of the matter by asking questions. If you do not stop passive aggressive behaviors and tendencies early, they will turn into a pattern of communication you may not be able to get out of later on, so address the issue early and you will be much happier and have healthier conversations in the long run.

Because passive aggressive communication style is so prevalent it is important to watch for it in all of your communications with friends, family members, spouses, and, most of all, your children. Let's break this unhealthy pattern of communication and really say what we mean!

The world is full of a multitude of eccentric personalities from the neurotic to those with eating disorders and we must be able to live with them all. Each and every one of us will have some form of unbalanced behavior and may even demonstrate some of these conditions ourselves. What we must watch out for is when our behaviors or the behaviors of those around us cross over the line from a healthy neuroses to a damaging neurotic behavior.

Therapy is available to help people become better adjusted to society and allow them to manage their differences as they go through life and engage with the rest of the world.

If we all work together and support each other we can help everyone to live healthy lives and take joy in our differences. After all, the world would be a very boring place if each one of us were exactly alike!

While we know that just because we have explained and provided examples of the different types of people in the world, it does not mean that everyone will get along. But at least with knowledge, there is power and maybe this book will help someone to be more understanding and build a relationship with his or her fellow mentally ill person.

Other books by author on Kindle, paperback and audio

Creating Good Habits Breaking Bad Habits: Learn How To Transform Your Life Completely By Developing Good Habits And Eliminating Bad Habits